M000074367

How We Got Over:

Testimonies of Faith, Hope, and Courage

How We Got Over:

Testimonies of Faith, Hope, and Courage

Edited by
Dr. Trevy A. McDonald
and
Dr. Bettye J. Allen

Foreword by
Dr. M. Joan Cousin
Episcopal Supervisor
Fourth Episcopal District
African Methodist Episcopal Church

Reyomi Publishing
Chicago

For Marilyn
Keep the faith through steadfast
hope and you will stay
encouraged!
Trevy A. McDonald

This book is dedicated to:

The children who were left behind on the continent of Africa, due to the AIDS Pandemic.

CONTENTS

Testimonies of Hope

Testimonies of Courage

Listening to Our Elders

Foreword

by Dr. M. Joan Cousin
Episcopal Supervisor
Women's Missionary Society
Fourth Episcopal District
African Methodist Episcopal Church

We all face challenges in life; health challenges, employment challenges, and personal challenges. Through our faith in God, hope for a better and brighter tomorrow, and courage to face the future, we as a people have been able to maintain strength in the struggle.

Just like our ancestors were guided through prayer, we as a people have made it. No matter how difficult the road may be, keep your faith in God, stay focused on Him and you too will make it.

I was taught early in life by my parents who were God-loving and God-fearing Christians, to keep my focus on God. When you stay focused on God, He will lead you to places, people and situations you never imagined.

In 1976 my husband was elected to the Episcopacy of the AME Church. My new role included not only being a Missionary, but Supervisor of Missions for the Ninth Episcopal District (Alabama). After spending eight years in Alabama, we were assigned to the Eleventh Episcopal District which includes Florida and the Bahamas. In 1985, I became involved in the AIDS struggle. It was not popular at that time, but I felt like I had to do something to make a difference. I was compelled to save people. While our mission in the Christian Church is to win souls for Christ, my platform became — if you can't save a body, how can you save a soul?

When I first became involved in AIDS activism, I was treated as if I had lost my mind. I was called crazy but not because I had been diagnosed with a mental disorder. I was called crazy because people were afraid of the truth. Discussions of sex in the church were, and still are taboo despite what was and still is going on. The bottom line was that people didn't want to change their behavior.

In 1986 the first AIDS station opened in Miami. I began to learn more about the virus. Over the next several years I read numerous books including *And the Band Played On* and *Idol, Rock Hudson: The True Story of an American Film Hero.* I also enrolled in classes for two years. These were free classes that were open and available to the public. The classes, while informative, weren't well attended. Yet despite my enhancement of knowledge about this deadly disease, I was still persecuted and wanted to give up the struggle.

I found both inspiration and motivation from eight simple words from my youngest son Joseph who said, "Mom, if not you, who? If not now, when?" That was the encouragement I needed to maintain strength in the struggle.

In 1987, armed with the shield of knowledge about HIV/AIDS and the willingness to spread my knowledge, I spoke at the Quadrennial meeting of the Women's Missionary Society of the African Methodist Episcopal Church. Sadly the predictions of that time have come true. AIDS is now a pandemic. The United States is paralleling Southern Africa in AIDS cases. People are dying all around us and we act like we don't know what's going on because we are afraid.

We're afraid of other's opinions.

We're afraid that we'll lose everything .

We're afraid to admit the truth.

We're afraid because we never called it what it is.

It is AIDS, and according to the United Nations *Report on the Global HIV/AIDS Epidemic 2002,* since the pandemic began, more than 60 million people have been infected with the virus.[1] Twenty million have died since the first clinical evidence of AIDS/HIV was reported and forty million live with the disease globally. I use the word reported here, because there are those who are still afraid. They don't get tested for HIV and they continue to spread the virus. According to 2002 statistics, approximately one in every 100 adults between the ages of 15 and 49 is infected.

AIDS affects more than the individual who contracts the HIV virus. Over 14 million children globally are orphans as a result of the pandemic, 80 percent who live in sub-Saharan Africa. In South Africa, it is estimated that by 2010 there will be 1.5 million children orphaned as a result of the AIDS pandemic. Botswana is now the epicenter of the HIV Virus. According to 2001 statistics, one out of every three children is HIV positive. In 2000 there were 68,000 AIDS orphans in Botswana alone, a country with a population of 1.7 million. We must open our eyes and see that this pandemic is real. This pandemic is a destroyer of life and of livelihood. This pandemic is a silent killer, to which we must respond.

We must band together to save bodies. For when we save bodies, we can nurture, educate, and empower others so that we can save souls! It is up to us to make this difference.

---

[1] Joint United Nations Programme on HIV/AIDS. (2002, July). *Report on the Global HIV/AIDS Epidemic 2002.*

If we don't band together and do it, it is an utter disgrace to Him who made us.

While this book project was conceptualized to raise funds to support AIDS orphans in Southern Africa, it is not about making money. *How We Got Over: Testimonies of Faith, Hope and Courage* is about helping people to realize their fullest potential and enjoy an abundant life if they just stay focused on God. If we can save one, we can save the nation. AIDS is now the leading cause of death among African women of childbearing age. Half of all HIV infections worldwide occur in women in Africa. If the women are gone, then the race is gone. We are focusing on the African continent because this is from whence we came, and when Africa is gone, the world will exist no more.

Blacks across the Diaspora have always faced challenges, and we have always survived because of our tenacity, persistence, and perseverance. As Marcus Garvey said, "Look for me in the whirlwind or the storm, look for me all around you, for, with God's grace, I shall come and bring with me countless millions of black slaves who have died in America and the West Indies and the millions in Africa to aid you in the fight for Liberty, Freedom and Life."

We will survive, as we have, because of our faith, our focus and our purpose; and we will tell the story for generations to come...how we got over.

Acknowledgments

On behalf of the contributors and editors, we first thank God for all of His many blessings and for strengthening us through our every day experiences. Thanks to Bishop Philip R. Cousin for his support of this project as well as the Presiding Elders, local Pastors, Missionaries, and laypersons who have publicized, promoted and participated in this project.

The editors wish to thank all those who assisted by sharing their stories for this volume. The contributors were both numerous and generous in sharing their stories with us and supporting this cause. While some of the contributors desired to have bylines attached to their stories, others requested to have their names listed alphabetically in acknowledgment.

We thank the following contributors: Dr. Anne Barton, Michelle D. Belle-Villa, Sallie Bolton, Sharon J. Brumfield, Carolyn Burgess, Brett E. Chambers, Earline Clark, Naomi Clay, Geneva Coleman, Valerie Cousin, Evelyn E. Farris, Annie Marie Ford, Pearla Gholston, Norma Gibbs, Jurlene Glover, Julia Hagwood, Allena Henderson, Hallie B. Hendrieth-Smith, Mary Fleming Hughes, Betty Louise Hyter, Marina Jackson, Ruth E. James, Evelyn Jefferson, Aj D. Jemison, Elaine B. Johnson, Rosalind Marie Kennedy, Bertha Ford Keys, Marjorie Kimbrough, Mary F. Laws, Franc Levion, Beverly Mahone, Patricia Mathis, Michele Matthews, Jacquelin McCord, Thomas L. McDonald, Sr., Jewel E. Orr-Jones, Norma J. Phillips, C.L. Poindexter, Ethel Powell, Dr. B.J. Primus-Cotton, Mattie Ramsey, Pauline M. Rivers, Lorenzo C. Robertson, J. Ricc Rollins, II, Nona Skiby, Dana Burns Smith, Joan Stigler, Irma M. Williams, Jacqueline Williams, and DeAnne S. Winey-Ward.

We would also like to thank Thomas L. McDonald, Sr. and Ricc Rollins for their assistance in selecting scriptures for some of the stories.

A special thanks to Teresa Fowler for her editing expertise, Charlene Thompson, Esq. for her support and legal advice, and Robert Montgomery, CPA for his guidance.

Reyomi Publishing wishes to thank all of the booksellers, book reviewers, book clubs and individual readers for continued support of our publications.

Introduction

It is both a blessing and an honor to co-edit this volume of testimonies. *How We Got Over* is evidence to God's power, and how, if you remain faithful and put your trust in Him, He will order your steps and guide your paths.

In the summer of 1999, shortly after I started Reyomi Publishing, my mother and I enjoyed a Sunday afternoon on our front porch. It was on this afternoon that I shared plans for a new book project with her. My idea was to publish a book of Testimonies, "but only if it will support a charity." While the idea was grand, I put it on the backburner and pursued other interests.

About a year later I attended the Chicago Annual Conference at Brown Chapel African Methodist Episcopal Church in Joliet, IL as a book vendor. I took the opportunity to introduce myself to our newly assigned Episcopal Supervisor who asked about my products. After a brief discussion she learned that I had a publishing company and shared the *How We Got Over* book project with me. I was in awe as I recalled the conversation I had with my mother. Along with Dr. Bettye J. Allen and the numerous contributors who shared their testimonies, this project moved from an idea in the heads of two women who had never met, to a book proposal and now to a finished product. Monies from *How We Got Over: Testimonies of Faith, Hope and Courage* will support the children orphaned by the AIDS Pandemic in Southern Africa. The center in Botswana provides counseling, testing, after-school tutoring, and meals for hundreds of children orphaned by the pandemic. The South African centers have served over 300,000 clients in the Western Cape since 1999, providing similar services.

The significance of recalling *How We Got Over* serves as a sharpening piece to our gratitude. It is easy at times to forget from whence we came. Reflecting on *How We Got Over* also serves as an inspiration to others and especially to young people.

This dynamic and spirit-filled collection opens with a foreword written by Dr. Cousin, which chronicles her journey as an AIDS activist since 1985. Her mission work for this cause spans the globe.

Based on proverbs, human attitude, and nature, Adinkra symbols have served to share messages of faith, hope, courage, and remembering our past. These symbols are used throughout the book as a guide to reflecting on how we got over.

Every moment of each day is an exercise in faith. From the most basic daily functions such as breathing to sustain life, to trusting God's plan and will for our lives, faith is demonstrated. Nyame nti, the Adinkra symbol of faith and trust in God is a river plant known as Adwera. This symbol serves as a remembrance of God's power in stories such as "Do You Have Faith?" where two people survived being submerged in water while trapped inside an automobile in the aftermath of a deadly hurricane. Other contributors have shared stories of miraculous healing from life-threatening illnesses, the survival and protection of their children, and how the faith instilled in them during childhood has enabled them to make it over. It is through faith and watching God work in our lives that we have hope.

Like faith, hope sustains us while we are continuing to trust God to work as only He can. "Nyame biribi wo soro," the Adinkra symbol for hope, reminds us that God's dwelling place is in the heavens where he can listen to all prayers. A woman, newly married to her companion and best friend of seven years was ecstatic to learn she would be a mother, but shocked when her water broke at twenty weeks gestation. Despite the statistics and the odds of her child's survival, she remained strong in faith and hopeful. While her daughter only lived seven hours, she served as an angel of unity and strength in her family. Broken relationships were healed and a family once estranged was reunited. Through divorce, trying times, and meager starts God's promises give us hope for a new tomorrow.

"Nya akokooduro," the Adinkra symbol for courage reminds us that courage enables us to remove the obstacles that stand in our way. Through courage, we are able to turn stumbling blocks into stepping stones as we pursue the unattainable and use our lives as a testimony to make a difference in the life of another. Testimonies of miracles, healing emotional wounds and overcoming abusive relationships, in the courage section are uplifting and empowering.

Sankofa, the symbol of the importance of learning from the past, reminds us that we should listen to our elders. Not only have they paved the way through prayer, but through their experiences we learn a wealth of information, receive inspiration and become confident that we too, will make it over.

This collection closes with a voice from the continent of Africa. Sarah Nkele Matlhare shares her experience of providing support and supplies for those infected and affected by the AIDS pandemic in Botswana where one in three children is infected with HIV and 68,000 orphans struggle to survive in a country with a population of 1.7 million.

The cover photo, taken in the early 1920s, makes a statement about where we, as a people, started. Through the support of our churches, communities, immediate and extended families, we have been able to pave the way for future generations. When we reflect on our past and look at what our ancestors endured, we know with a certainty that if we keep the faith, and embrace the legacy and courage of those who traveled before us, our divine destiny is imminent.

Each of the stories in this collection is true and original. Contributors range from widely published authors, to everyday people with a story to tell. This book is evidence of the words in James 1:2-3, "Consider it pure joy, my brothers, whenever you face trials of many kinds, because you know that the testing of your faith develops perseverance." (NIV).

On behalf of my co-editor, it is my hope that *How We Got Over: Testimonies of Faith, Hope and Courage* will lift you when you're down, motivate you when you're still, and empower you when you feel weak.

Trevy A. McDonald, Ph.D.

Faith

Do You Have Faith?
by Brett Chambers

Thy faith hath saved thee; go in peace.
Luke 7:50 (KJV)

Do you have faith? It is a question we're often asked, but how often do we think about what it really means. In 1999 I experienced a life-changing trauma where, along each step of the way, an act of faith enabled me to survive.

After a 20-year career in broadcast media I found myself in graduate school and surviving on a series of freelance production jobs. On Thursday September 17, 1999, I was contacted by an independent production company. My job for the next several days was to shoot video for Carolina Power & Light (CP & L) in some of the areas devastated by Hurricane Floyd which came through Eastern North Carolina the prior two days. Floyd, a category three hurricane with winds up to 130 miles per hour, was 580 miles wide. When Floyd hit the coast of North Carolina and dumped between 15 and 20 inches of rain in some areas of the state, residents had just begun to recover from Hurricane Dennis ten days earlier, which left six inches of rain.

Along with a Cindy Carter, a freelance producer, I was to acquire and archive video for use in training, marketing, and public relations. It seemed like a simple and routine assignment, shooting video of restoration efforts including pictures of the damage, the CP & L employees offering relief and aid to those directly affected, and the restoration of power lines. This routine assignment turned into a life altering experience.

When I met Cindy, a petite, eclectic woman with colorful hair, we did not know we were expected to use our own vehicles for the shoot. My van needed work, as did Cindy's car, so we decided to rely on the comfort of a rental vehicle rather than driving our personal vehicles.

When we arrived at the airport rental facility, we requested a sport utility vehicle and the rental agent offered a relatively new Isuzu Trooper. When he asked me about purchasing insurance I jokingly agreed to purchase the insurance that would cover the vehicle if I returned without the keys. At the time I didn't realize that this decision was only one small part of my preparation for what was to become.

I loaded my belongings, all of my research not only my master's thesis, but for every class I was taking that semester, my trumpet, clothing for a few days, my personal mini-DV Video Camera and my bicycle flashlight into the Emerald Green Isuzu Trooper along with the equipment from the production company. Cindy and I were on our way to a shoot that was to last for three days.

Goldsboro, North Carolina was our first stop. When we arrived in the city, we observed some standing water, but all-in-all it didn't look that bad. We watched kids riding their bicycles in water that came up to their seats in the parking lot of a day care center. While strange and interesting, we just chalked it up to a fearless act of play.

We stopped not far from the parking lot to shoot what is known in the industry as "B-Roll" of trees which had been uprooted as a result of Floyd, downed power lines and flooding—normal hurricane aftermath. We started out using the production company's camera, but there was no battery in the recently repaired camera. My mini DV camera came in handy.

After shooting some footage, we got back into the Trooper and began driving through Goldsboro. As we drove down Royall Avenue, we saw standing water in the road and decided to turn around. After shooting what we could, we decided to go to our second stop, New Bern, North Carolina.

Not knowing the way to New Bern, we stopped at a convenience store for supplies and directions. We were told the way we could go if the hurricane's devastation hadn't closed roads. Royall Avenue was recommended to us so we headed in that direction.

After tuning the radio to the audio channel for NBC to hear *Frasier*, we noticed that Royall Avenue was now completely dry. I used the yellow lines in the street as my guide for staying on my side of the road. After 9 p.m., it was very dark outside and because the power lines were down as a result of Hurricane Floyd, there were no streetlights. As we drove down the incline the water got higher and eventually the yellow lines disappeared.

"Brett, we're in water!" Cindy exclaimed as I looked to my sides and above me. The current from the floodwater had washed away the earth and asphalt beneath the bridge and our two ton rental vehicle was heading down, engine first into the water.

"Do you have faith?" I asked Cindy.

"Yes. Now what?"

Quickly I rolled the windows down and unlocked the doors. I knew that everything, windows, door locks, etc., were electronic in the vehicle and we had to act quickly before the water shorted out the electricity.   I was even more concerned that we had been charging batteries in the center of the front seat and the possibility of electrocution entered my mind.

"If we have faith we won't panic, if we panic we're dead."

"OK Brett," Cindy said as I helped her get out of the vehicle to safety.

It is often said that one sees their entire life flash before them during near death experiences. I had a flashback of a Boy Scout camp activity.   While fully clothed, we were instructed to jump into the water and remain for what seemed like an eternity.

"Relax, don't panic. It's not the water that kills you, it's the panic," were the words I heard my Boy Scout Camp Counselor telling me.   The water was just below my nostrils, I was completely submerged, and it was dark. My door was slightly ajar as I stuffed my cell phone, pager and bicycle flashlight into my shirt. Calmly but earnestly trying to get out of the vehicle, I found myself stuck. "It's not the water that kills you, it's the panic," were the words I heard once again. Relax Brett, don't panic. I tried again to get out of the vehicle but couldn't move far when I realized I had forgotten to unfasten my seatbelt. As I was swimming away from the vehicle my glasses were washed away. I have a difficult enough time seeing without my glasses in the daylight, with blackness surrounding me my vision was not impaired, it was impossible.

Fortunately, the water was even with the bridge so I easily found the surface. "Cindy, where are you?" I called when I didn't see or hear her on the bridge. I removed the bicycle flashlight from my shirt and saw that she was still in the water, on the other side of the truck. After I got her to safety we took inventory. We were in shock! How did it happen and how did we survive?

I didn't realize at the time how pertinent my question, "Do you have faith?" was but it was a mere act of faith along each step of the way that enabled Cindy and me to survive. Enveloped in darkness without my glasses, through faith I reached up and pulled myself to safety. I was able to save Cindy because I had brought a waterproof flashlight rather than my regular flashlight.

As we stood on the bridge shivering and immersed in darkness I saw a light in the other direction. I flashed my flashlight and a police officer who was barricading the road on the opposite side of the bridge from which we were driving called to us, asked if we were all right and then radioed for a search and rescue team.

The firefighters assisted Cindy to the boat, as by now the water was up to the thigh of my 6'5" frame. They first offered to take us to the hospital—actually they encouraged us to be taken to the hospital. We refused. We wanted to get home as soon as possible but Raleigh-Durham was not in their jurisdiction. They offered their regrets and instead took us to the Carolina Power & Light Command Post.

Once I reached safety and warmth, I had another thought provoking experience. I sat in the Command Post where the gracious employees offered us food, dry clothing, and warm blankets and thought about whom I should call. Not wanting to alarm my parents at the time, I decided not to call them. I sat there and thought about all of the friends and relatives who had me listed as their emergency contact, but I had no one. I tried to reach my daughter but she wasn't home. Neither was my pastor.

My portable life—my entire semester's work including thesis-related research, clothing, trumpet, and video camera—were with me on the trip. They got submerged, but I resurged. I was fortunate to be alive.

When I returned to the comfort of my home and showered vigorously, I made special note not to turn on the television. I wanted some peace and solitude. As I sat down and checked my e-mail, Miriam Thomas, a news anchor and close friend, was on-line and asked me if I had time to talk. When she called, she told me how taxing the evening had been. She and her co-anchor had remained on-the-air following the newscast because there were two search and rescue helicopters out trying to locate missing people from the storm. When Miriam finished relaying this information to me she asked how I was doing. I told her I was almost the third search and rescue team, and then gave her the details of my night.

Two days later, Cindy returned to Goldsboro with another cameraman to complete the shoot. She went to the site where our rental vehicle was submerged and noticed that the water level had receded greatly. A police officer told her she had to leave the area because of the danger and began telling her about what happened Thursday night.
"I know," Cindy said. "I was in the vehicle."

"See the tags there?" the officer asked. "That's your vehicle there."

"It isn't," Cindy replied. "Our vehicle was a rental and the tag number started with a 'R.' This one starts with a 'G.'"

It was then, two days later, that the authorities realized another driver had the fateful experience of being submerged. Sadly, this person was still in the vehicle. She left her home on Thursday to check on her mother. Due to the storm, telephone lines weren't operating so her family thought she had arrived at her mother's. As far as her mother knew, she was at home with her family. No one knew to look for her because no one knew she was missing.

Sunday while in church, my pastor asked me to testify about my experience, which I did reluctantly. It was fresh in my mind, but I wasn't ready to relive it. After church I checked my messages on the cell phone and had been called to the station where I once worked for an interview. During the interview, the reporter played footage of the area where the rental vehicle went under and the car which was discovered on Saturday being recovered. I was amazed to learn that someone else experienced the same fate as Cindy and me, only this person wasn't fortunate enough to survive.

While leaving the station I ran into Tony Debo, a sports reporter who survived a helicopter crash a few years earlier. He relayed to me that he had been having recurring dreams about falling from the sky. I too had been having recurring dreams about flying down the street to save someone. Our dreams ended when we experienced our trauma.

The following Sunday after church I stopped by *Starbucks* and picked up a copy of the *Raleigh News & Observer*, which featured coverage of the hurricane. In the middle of a page was a picture and small feature on the woman in the car that was recovered the previous Saturday. I grabbed my latte, the newspaper and went home to read the story in my solitude.

While reading the paper, something came over me and I was led to look her mother up and contact her. She and I were born the same year, she and my daughter share the same birthdate, and she was married and the mother of two children. When I spoke to her mother I was able to provide some details about her daughter's death that only Cindy or I could provide. It brought her some closure.

Five months later, while on a retreat where I was assisting a friend in Puerto Rico, I spent some time reflecting and journaling on a legal pad about my experience. My reflections became a letter to God, which included confession, concerns, and how this experience shaped me. When I finished this letter, I balled it up and put it into the ocean. It was then that I felt a weight lifted from me.

 Everything Will Be All Right

"Everything will be all right," were the words uttered by my spouse on January 31, 1975 when our first child was born three months premature—weighing one pound and twelve ounces. Several doctors, along with many nurses were in attendance. This was an unbelievable situation since many people feel a six-month baby does not survive.

My husband and I had been praying unceasingly for a child, knowing that if we would keep the faith, "everything will be all right." There were whispers among persons gathered due to our baby being so small. In fact, we were told by my attending physician not to expect our baby to live through the night.

When we saw our baby, I exclaimed, "That baby is breathing." It was a fact, he was seemingly "gasping." I immediately went into prayer and asked God to take care of him because we had faith he would survive.

In addition to the low weight, many complications set in. We were told there were several possibilities: retardation, brain damage, even mongolism. Neither exist in my son, Praise God!

He graduated with high honors from high school and received several scholarships. He served as President of the Conference Branch YPD (Young People's Department) and as the Fourth Episcopal District President. At present, he is a Connectional YPD Officer and a member of the General Board. Faith did this!

We praise God for crowning our son with these victories, especially since we were unable to hold him until he was a month old. We were not privileged to name our son until he was two days old. He has earned a Bachelor's degree, as well as a Master's degree.

These accomplishments are based on our philosophy. "Everything will be all right" (through faith). When we humbly observed our son's successes, we realized God has given us a faith that will not shrink.

He Always Makes a Way
by Earline D. Clark

Let all who run to you for protection
always sing joyful songs.
Provide shelter for those who truly love you
and let them rejoice.
Psalm 5:11 (CEV)

In the winter of 1963 my husband of 11 years lost his job. We were the parents to four lovely children. At that time, in order to receive assistance from the government, a parent was obligated to work. Since I was qualified for clerical work, I was told to work for the University of Chicago.

After being there for three months I was hired permanently. I ended up being employed by the University for 32 years. My husband was called back to work after a short period of time.

Naturally, in the beginning we were discouraged, but I prayed about it and trusted God. Somehow, someway, I knew that He would make a way and He did.

Oh, thank You God and praise Your name forever.

God's Amazing Grace
by Joan Stigler

(For the LORD thy God is a merciful God;) he will not forsake thee, neither destroy thee, nor forget the covenant of thy fathers which he sware unto them.
Deuteronomy 4:31 (KJV)

When I was 20, my 43-year-old mother died of a cerebral hemorrhage. Because I felt she was too young to die I turned away from the very God my mother had taught me to serve. I stopped attending church, Sunday School and I even stopped reading my Bible.

During this dark period in my life, I suffered from headaches, body aches and all kinds of pain. When the doctors couldn't find anything wrong with me I became angry with them.

About a year after my mother's death, I picked up my Bible, began reading scripture and I began praying, asking God to forgive me. I realized in my darkest hour, God was still shedding His grace and mercy upon me.

This was the turning point in my faith walk. To realize that God was protecting me, even while I was angry with Him, brought home what God's Amazing Grace really means.

Miracles are Possible
by **Allena Henderson**

Then Jesus answered and said unto her, O woman, great is thy faith: be it unto thee even as thou wilt. And her daughter was made whole from that very hour.
Matthew 15:28 (KJV)

My granddaughter only weighed one pound and 11 ounces when she was born prematurely. The doctor did a C-Section and said he didn't know if she would make it.

I said, "There is a God who can do all things."

A specialist for premature babies was called in. She asked me, "Do you believe in what God can do?" My friend and I went into the nursery and knelt down by my granddaughter's incubator and prayed.

On that Sunday morning I had to drive 60 miles from Waterloo where they had the neonatal intensive care unit because I knew there was a God. My granddaughter is now a high school senior.

A Shared Answer for a Prayer of Healing
by Mattie P. Ramsey

Because he turned his ear to me,
I will call on him as long as I live.
Psalm 116:2 (NIV)

During our early ministry and the height of the Civil Rights Movement in Cairo, Illinois, we had been blessed with two children, a boy and a girl. The little girl became sick with allergies and required special foods and liquid *Sobee Milk* (a soybean milk).

We had very few funds and the fact that we were involved in Civil Rights did not help our source of funds. The special foods my daughter required cost a tremendous amount of money and we ran up a large drug and milk bill at a pharmacy in Cairo.

Because of our involvement in the Civil Rights Movement, the pharmacy closed our account because we could not pay as projected. One day I called for liquid *Sobee Milk* and the pharmacist refused my request. That day at church we had mid-week prayer service. I prayed for the health of my daughter and I believed that God would hear and answer my prayer.

He did hear my prayer. This day ended her need for additional medicine or liquid *Sobee Milk*. God was my angel of mercy.

My daughter lived until she was 38 years old and she gave her short life to the Lord. She raised her two children to believe in God and the power of prayer. Today we have two exceptional grandchildren for whom we are well blessed.

Sufficient Grace
by Rachelle Hollie Guillory

And he said unto me, My grace is sufficient for thee: for my strength is made perfect in weakness. Most gladly therefore will I rather glory in my infirmities, that the power of Christ may rest upon me.
2 Corinthians 12:9 (KJV)

Have you ever considered your position in the Kingdom? Why were you called? Why were you chosen? What is your purpose? What is God's plan for your life? Why are you here? The cares of life will definitely cause you to pose these questions to yourself. If I am experiencing such pain, why was I even born? Was I born solely to endure tribulation, grief and strife and a splash of happiness here and there. Have you ever suffered the "Why Me?" syndrome. Often when one falls into the stupor of sorrowfulness, one typically fails to count the many mercies extended by God's grace--Discounting the fact that grace is given without merit. Truthfully the question one should ask is, "Why not me?"

You and I were chosen by God before the foundation of the world. (Ephesians 1:4) God knows our end from our beginning. Your life's book has already been written. However, it is now being read openly by you and everyone you encounter during your life's journey. In some way during each person's life, the purpose God has for you will be fulfilled—for He already knew the path you would take. Knowing that if I walk uprightly before God, then He will not withhold any good thing from me.   (Psalm 84:11) Believing that if God's thoughts of me are good and not evil, then He will bring about an expected end for me (Jeremiah 29:1) and, resting in the fact that I love God and I am the called according to his purpose, then all things will work for my good. (Romans 8:28) Knowing these truths, believing these truths and resting in these truths, is How I Got Over! Despite the many ailments that afflicted my body, I knew that God's grace was sufficient.

As a child I suffered many injustices; familial as well as social.   Although social injustices are painful, the scars caused by familial injustices are tremendously heartrending and often much more difficult to liberate one's self from. Scarred permanently by the hand of a grandparent (both physically and mentally), I know all too well why the caged bird sings.   However, God comes to transform us by the renewing of our minds. These injustices I faced are part of the reason my mother called me strong.

Assuming that these scars, in my mind, were healed, I thought I was okay. Until one beautiful summer Monday in June of 1994—I began to hemorrhage. Having gone back and forth to the emergency room more than four times in two days, I finally collapsed on the porch of my home after returning home at 12:30 a.m. from another emergency visit Wednesday morning. At this point, any blood that came from my body was now clear with a pink tinge.   The question, "Why Me?" was looming in my mind. I have heard people speak of out-of-body experiences, but I never pondered their validity. As I lay on the cold cement porch, I felt nothing. My body was numb. What I felt was strange. I was actually disconnected from the body of flesh which had contained my soul and spirit.

Just drifting above my body, I began to speak to the Lord. I heard my husband (I have since divorced) saying, "You must really be sick because there are water bugs crawling around you and you're not moving." I told Jesus that I wanted to live so that I could raise my two beautiful children. I promised Him that I would continue to raise them as God-fearing and God-loving individuals. My request was that He would allow me to live so that I could raise my children. They needed me. The presence of God is awesome. He met me there. A peace that is indescribable encased me. Just as suddenly as my spirit felt disconnected from my frail body, my spirit was re-connected with my flesh. I thanked God because at that point I knew I would be just fine. It did not really mater what would occur next. God's presence comforted me.

I crawled into my house and asked my husband to call 9-1-1. I was taken by ambulance to the emergency room of a hospital near my home. Two IVs were inserted in my arms because I was told my hemoglobin count (a protein and main component of red blood cells carrying oxygen from and to the lungs) was a 5.5; it is supposed to be 12.1 to 15.1 in females. Consequently, the doctors would need to supply my body with blood expeditiously. Unfortunately, my insurance provider would not cover my visit there. I was transported via ambulance to the hospital of which I was covered. The hurriedness of the emergency room staff caused me some concern. I had to pray and exercise my faith. As the paramedics pushed my bed through the emergency doors, about five to seven members of the emergency room staff were waiting for me. I knew I was gravely ill when I heard them ask, "Is this the 5.5?" Also, the fact that so many of the staff members were in one place, at one time, giving attention to one person caused me more concern.

As a potassium-filled fluid traveled through my veins via the IVs, my body was being fooled to believe that blood was flowing through it. Consequently, I began to feel a little better. Numerous doctors came to visit me that early morning. The first one told me that I needed to have a blood transfusion—at least three to four units of blood. I told him that I did not want a transfusion. A second doctor visited me and told me that I needed a blood transfusion. I told her that I did not want one. Finally a third doctor came into my room. Before he could talk I asked him why I felt needle prickling sensations in my extremities. He told me it was because I did not have any blood left in my arms and legs. He said that most of the blood in my body was now in my brain area. This doctor told me that the other doctors did not want to alarm me. "But," he said, "you are going to die if you don't get a blood transfusion." The doctors believed the cause of my hemorrhaging was due to multiple fibroid tumors in my uterus. I asked if I could have the hysterectomy without having the blood. He told me that without a transfusion of at least four units of blood, they would be unable to save me after their first cut to my body.

"Why don't you want a blood transfusion," he asked me. "Because I do not want to contract the AIDS virus," was my reply to him. His next and strategic question was, "Why don't you want to get AIDS?" "Because I don't want to die," I told him. "Well," he said, "I assure you that you will die tonight if you don't get this blood transfusion." However, he said, if you get AIDS from this blood you will at least have some more years to live. He told me that I would have to sign a release form stating that I know that I will die without the blood transfusion—thereby releasing the hospital of any liability.

As a Christian, I thought I should not get sick, at least not to this degree. As a Christian, I thought my faith would make this situation disappear. As a Christian, I thought I did something really terrible for God to allow me to suffer through this. Yes, I thought, why me? Why not? God reminded me that Paul sought the Lord thrice! I asked the emergency room staff if I could make a few calls before I agree to the blood transfusion. Because I would die, they said, if I lost any more blood, the staff pushed my bed from the room to the nurses' station so that I could use the phone. I called my mother and my pastor and asked them what did they think about my getting a blood transfusion. My pastor said there was no biblical substantiation for my declining the transfusion and my mother yelled at me and told me to, "Take that blood, girl!"

My sister arrived at the hospital just in time to pray over the blood with me. We held the blood and prayed God's blessing and anointing over it. Then, she and I sang praise and worship songs as the blood traveled through my body. The next morning I went into surgery for the emergency hysterectomy.

What is my testimony, you ask. During the eleven-hour surgery, my doctor found another growth in my intestines. Unbeknownst to them, this was the actual growth that was causing my hemorrhaging. While she left me open, my doctor called in a specialist to diagnose the growth she thought was a tumor. I was diagnosed with Meckel's diverticulum. Only two percent of the population has Meckel's diverticulum, which is a "remnant of developmental structures that were not fully absorbed during fetal development" and it can cause bleeding in the intestines. Hemorrhaging is one of the complications of Meckel's diverticulum. Yes, had I not had the hysterectomy, the doctors may never have known that I had this condition. I most likely would have died before the doctors discovered this tumor in my intestine, which caused the excessive bleeding. Yes, to God be the glory! My faith was being tested. But as Job, I said yet will I trust Him.

Although I was criticized by someone for not having faith enough that God would provide me with a blood transfusion himself and not the doctors, and although I myself felt that I must have done something wrong to deserve this trauma and test, I held on to my faith in God. Some of us put too much faith in the power of doctors. I believe that if it was God's plan for me to die, I would be dead regardless of what procedure the doctor performed. The power of life and death is in the hands of God. Therefore, whether we see a doctor or not, God's will shall be fulfilled in us. I had faith that God would guide the doctor's hands and I would survive the surgery. Yes, I had faith that God would carry me through my trial, hope that I would see a brighter tomorrow, and courage to make it through whatever storm God allowed me to endure.

God comforted me with this scripture and to this day I quote it during my testing times: (2 Corinthians 12:8-10) "For this thing I besought the Lord thrice, that it might depart from me. And he said unto me, My grace is sufficient for thee: for my strength is made perfect in weakness. Most gladly therefore will I rather glory in my infirmities, that the power of Christ may rest upon me. Therefore I take pleasure in infirmities, in reproaches, in necessities, in persecutions, in distresses for Christ's sake: for when I am weak, then am I strong." This scripture is my testament of faith, hope and courage. Whatever my plight, it is well with my soul!

During your testing times, know that God's grace is sufficient. For you gain strength through your weakness! Walk in Sufficient Grace!

Through the Laundering
by Dr. Anne Barton

Blessed is the people that know the joyful sound: they shall walk, O LORD, in the light of thy countenance.
Psalm 89:15 (KJV)

Author Jack Kornfield's book, *After the Ecstasy, the Laundry*, gives the following quote from Julian Norwich. "If there be anywhere on earth a lover of God is safe I know nothing of it, for it was not shown to be. But this was shown, that in falling and rising again we are always kept in that same precious love."

The blessing of being an itinerant elder and pastor in the A.M.E. Church afforded me the privilege of making 23 consecutive annual conference pastoral reports representing wonderful people of several A.M.E. Churches. The pastorate was indeed an ecstatic and exhilarating experience despite the difficulties that kept one prayerfully alert as a visionary.

The vision did not reveal the catastrophe that brought embarrassment, shock, amazement, and incredulity all combined to bring a sense of great devastation. As unfulfilled promises prevailed, I stood on the annual conference floor anticipating a new promised appointment. Instead, I was left standing with disappointment, which precipitated mental anguish, physical illnesses, neurosis, and a spiritual crisis. Through anguish and sleepless nights I cried out "God, why? Where are you?" To whom could I go? My beloved husband had gone to be with the Lord. My one child could not understand. Friends asked unanswerable questions or suggested public or legal procedures from which I refrained.

I was never cowardly as some indicated. I have always loved our Zion, which presented me some wonderful experiences. I did not choose to reflect upon her unkindly. I also considered some younger female ministerial candidates in process whom I did not wish to be discouraged. But beyond this, I believed the Gospel I was preaching. "No safe place among men?" Perhaps. But continually on my knees, through despair, through the fall, God has kept me in His precious love. Only He could and did come to rescue me.

I praise Him for renewed health and vitality, for increased divine wisdom, and a forgiving spirit. I praise Him for the power and ministry and the many open doors He has given me for this hour. I now have a peace which the world can neither manufacture nor purchase.

How I got over! Jesus, you brought me all the way "through the laundering!" My prayer is Savior let me walk with Thee. My song is Amazing Grace.

Down Through the Years
by Bertha F. Keys

Trust in the Lord with all your heart
and lean not on your own understanding;
in all your ways acknowledge him,
and he will make your paths straight.
Proverbs 3:5-6 (NIV)

After finishing school, I married my high school sweetheart and we became parents to four children. Early in our marriage, we moved to Wisconsin where my husband, Julius, accepted the call to the ministry. During his ministry, I recall that we left several lovely homes to be assigned to churches in areas where we had nowhere to live. We have had to rely totally on the Lord for everything.

When my husband's employer relocated from Wisconsin to California, he had an option to move with it, but chose to remain in Wisconsin and trust the Lord to meet our needs rather than look for another job. This was a giant step in faith since our church only paid $35.00 a week. Although, after his job ended, the church gave him a five-dollar raise. That is when I really learned to trust in the Lord.

A few years later, the Bishop appointed us to a church in Minnesota, which paid $100.00 per week. We had to commute from Wisconsin to Minnesota for several months. During the commute, we stayed in the attic of one of our member's homes. When we were ready to move we had to sell our property. I prayed and asked the Lord if this was what he wanted us to do, to please help sell our home so that we could pay our debts and leave without being financially burdened. Without having put a sign in the yard or an ad in the newspaper, someone called asking to purchase our home within approximately four hours after my prayer. We sold our house to that person.

Since the new church did not have a parsonage, they found a house to rent and it later became their parsonage. We had extremely limited funds, but we continued to place our trust in God. During this time, we had one daughter entering college, and another in the fifth grade. Although we did not have money for college, God made a way for her to attend. She was able to live on campus for four years and received her Bachelor's degree.

These experiences proved to us that God can and will make a way out of no way, if you keep the faith. He is an on-time God

 # Eve's Renewal of Faith

He delivereth me from mine enemies: yea, thou liftest me up above those that rise up against me: thou hast delivered me from the violent man.
Psalm 18:48 (KJV)

Eve* had accepted Jesus Christ as her Savior as a teenager and joined an A.M.E. church where she is still a member. She became active in youth activities at church and completed her education, including graduate school. Her

---

* Not her real name

faithfulness in attending services and in practicing stewardship prepared her for her future marriage, but not in the way she had planned. Eve's husband was a machine technician who owned his business, but he did not practice the Catholic faith as he had when he was growing up.

Her joy in the Lord helped Eve to endure several years of verbal and physical abuse from her husband. The embarrassment of public and private incidents of abuse caused Eve to endure many days and nights of tears, prayers, and doubt about her self-esteem. Victims of abuse do not wish to discuss their problem with family or friends during the time of actual conflict. The police were called to the house once. Eve did consult the minister who married them and a mental health counselor. She went alone first and then convinced her husband to attend one session; he never returned for counseling, but Eve did.

Eve finally realized that the renewal of her faith reminded her that God had brought her through other valleys and would be the one to give her strength and peace to make the right decisions and avoid the power struggle with a paranoid person. She could rise above this horrible situation and be confident again in performing her college career and in growing spiritually without fear of what would happen to her.

Eve was reminded that she would not let anything separate her from the love of God. She also found comfort in reading Psalm 18, especially the verse, "He delivered her from the enemy — the violent man" and realized that after two trial separations, a permanent separation was necessary if she were going to survive with her life. God intervened in several ways to show her the steps to be taken for survival. She made a promise to God that if she did survive this tribulation she would serve Him through a deeper relationship. Just as God had kept his promises, Eve worked diligently to reach out to others in love. Instead of living in fear, Eve began to take on a new sense of peace and joy with a determination to get on with her life with God as the head. Her life has been wonderfully blessed through God's grace, which has opened many new doors.

Affirmation of Faith
by Geneva B. Coleman

Please pray to the LORD your God and ask him to heal my hand," Jeroboam begged. The prophet prayed, and Jeroboam's hand was healed.
1 Kings 13:6 (CEV)

If I would give my testimonies of the wondrous happenings in my life, they would make a mosaic-like quilt with many pieces woven together, testifying to the faith, hope, and courage God has given me. But I will share this one testimony of how God affirmed our faith and joy through a devastating accident.

My husband and I have one daughter and two sons, all of whom are very precious to us. When our daughter was ten-years-old, she was like most girls her age—busy and very energetic. She had a dog, Penny, who meant everything to her. She and the dog would play out in the yard for hours with each other. She believed she could do anything that Penny could do.

One beautiful afternoon, she and Penny were racing back and forth in our back yard, trying to see who was the fastest.

Well, as accidents happen, our daughter was running so fast that she could not stop as she came upon our back door, which was a glass storm door. She proceeded to put her hands out to stop herself and the door shattered, cutting both wrists, arms, nerve endings, veins, and other vital ligaments.

The doctors' outlook was grim after surgery and said that she may not ever be able to use her hands normally again. We never gave up hope as we prayed for God's healing. Today, when I look at my daughter I know that she was healed completely. The doctor gave all credit to the Lord and His miraculous healing power.

I am reminded of the miracle of faith and prayer, and know that He is always beside us in our darkest hour. I know that His promise is unchangeable and is forever.

A Doctor's Faith
by Sallie Bolton

To others the Spirit has given great faith or the power to heal the sick.
1 Corinthians 12:9 (KJV)

Three of my four children were accidentally poisoned by food they had eaten at a neighbor's home. Our four-year-old son was very sick as well as my two daughters. My husband and I took the children to the County Hospital. A friend of mine who was in the waiting room advised us to go to the hospital across the street. The waiting room was full and it would be a long wait before the doctor could see him.

We rushed our son to the other hospital. As the Lord would have it, there was no one in the waiting room. The pediatrician examined our son and advised us he had been poisoned. The doctor asked me how long he had been in a coma, of which I was not aware. I asked the doctor if my son was going to get well. He said, "I don't know. His temperature is 105 and his heartbeat is slow. All we can do is pray." Oh Lord how we prayed!

As they were preparing for my son's admission to the hospital I told my husband I could not watch my baby die. I told my husband to stay with my son, and I would get the girls from the County Hospital because they may also be poisoned.

I asked the pediatrician if he could examine my daughters. He was able to take the 12-year-old, but not the 13-year-old. I said I would bring both of the girls as there may be someone who would take care of the 13-year-old.

After a long stay in the hospital the girls came home first and then my son came home. I thank God for giving us back our children

He's Always Right on Time
by Sallie Bolton

After the death of the king of Egypt, the Israelites still complained because they were forced to be slaves. They cried out for help, and God heard their loud cries...
Exodus 2:23-24 (CEV)

One October the weather was getting very cold early. On one of these cold days I went to visit a friend. At that time, the coal man only delivered coal to my building monthly and that was the delivery day. My problem was that I didn't have enough money to get the coal that month. I only had ten dollars, and I needed that for groceries and carfare for my husband.

My friend said, "You have been so good to me that you can have the coal man bring you a ton and I'll give you the ten dollars."

I was so happy I ran home and told the coal man to bring me a ton of coal.

After he had put the coal in the house I went back to my friend's home to thank her for the money she was going to give me. She said, "I've been thinking since you left that it's getting cold and my kids need snowsuits, therefore I cannot let you have the money."

I was so disappointed that I went home and did the only thing I knew how. "Lord," I asked, "what am I going to do now?" I went to the mailbox and found a letter from a girl that my husband had sold some tickets to in June of that year.

She was apologizing for the delay in sending the money for the tickets. I got down on my knees and thanked God for the money. Now I had both carfare for my husband and groceries for my family.

Surgery of Faith
by Sadie W. Brooks

Peace I leave with you, my peace I give unto you: not as the world giveth, give I unto you. Let not your heart be troubled, neither let it be afraid
John 14:27 (KJV)

Fluid had been flowing from my nose for about six months. I had seen two specialists at the Ear, Nose and Throat Clinic, neither could resolve my problem. After seeing a neurologist at a local hospital, I needed surgery to correct the condition. After he explained to me the surgical process to stop the leaking of the fluid, I decided to proceed.

My husband and daughter were in the waiting room that morning in June 1996 for three hours while I was in surgery. The doctors had to cut my skull and lift my brain in order to repair some tissue that was torn.

My loved ones were upset that the surgery was taking so long. My friend came to the waiting room and told them everything was going to be all right.

During a post-operative visit I told the doctor the surgery took much longer than expected. The neurologist stated he didn't tell us the length of the surgery because he did not want us to worry too much.

I believe this was God's way of not giving me undo pressure before the surgery. He brought me through by faith. My friend was there to bring my husband and daughter comfort and compassion.

We're One in Christ
by Naomi M. Clay

So we, being many, are one body in Christ, and every one members one of another.
Romans 12:5 (KJV)

I believe in ecumenism. My experience several years ago made this a reality for me. Church Women United at that time had a program called *Causeways*, which consisted of trips to various parts of the world to see how women fared in different cultures. I was a part of a Caribbean Causeway.

Our group met in New York City for a basic briefing on what we might encounter. After a flight to Miami we separated into three groups and my group went to the Dominican Republic. Our leader was Sylvia Talbot, the current Episcopal Supervisor of the 13th District. At that time her husband was a pastor in the 16th District. The women were from several denominations throughout the country, including a nun and a woman of Indian descent. Only four of the women spoke Spanish, which was the official language of the country.

One day we went to a field where sugar cane was being cut by Haitians since they were willing to work so hard for only $3.00 a day. They were huge men who were desperate enough for money to feed themselves and send money to their families at home. When asked if they went to church, they responded they were A.M.E. and produced slips from their hats to prove it. It was heartwarming to see how these women responded to their needs, especially when they saw their living conditions.

We attended an A.M.E. Church where seating was on raised planks. The women heartily participated in the service even when the lights went out and candles had to be used. Their financial contributions were most rewarding and the worship so meaningful.

For the next two weeks, we visited villages and met women of such meager means who opened their hearts to us telling of their rigorous lives. The response of each woman to the experiences of that journey of faith made us one. Hearing their stories and seeing their faith in God humbled all of us and made our problems at home seem so trivial. I came home a changed woman having learned first hand that we are all the same in God's sight.

There is a God Somewhere

by J. Ricc Rollins, II

Let your conversation be without covetousness; and be content with such things as ye have: for he hath said, I will never leave thee, nor forsake thee.
Hebrews 13:5 (KJV)

I think that we often take life for granted and think that tomorrow is promised. If you asked anyone what they were going to do tomorrow or the next day, they would recite chapter and verse, pull out a Daytimer or Palm Pilot and give you a very detailed account of their plans. The operative word being, "their" plans. And much like most folk I too had plans for tomorrow, a tomorrow that almost didn't come.

I was traveling back from a morning speaking engagement with students from a Sarasota middle school. As I reflected on the morning and the more impressive students I smiled. Maybe the future was brighter than often projected. I left feeling like there was hope if youth and children alike embraced life and lived it to the fullest.

I traveled down the long stretch of highway and marveled at the beauty of the midday as I looked at the clock to see how I was doing on time. Once again I reflected on my schedule and the day before me. As the traffic came to a slow stop, I watched the traffic from the other side come to a stop as well. My attention was directed to a white car in the turn lane on the opposite side of the highway. I continued to watch as the light went through its paces. As the light turned green I said to myself, "This guy is going to cause an accident or hit somebody. Why is he trying to beat the traffic?" Before I could utter another word, the somebody the white car was going to hit, was me.

I can't tell you how, when or where I was hit, it was as if the world were painted white. The car struck me and I remember nothing else except for my gripping the steering wheel and hearing a voice say, "Don't steer, I've got this." I didn't respond. I just embraced the peace that filled my soul while whispering, "Okay, God it's on you."

I vaguely remember the first rotation of the car. An eyewitness later would tell the police that the car flipped three times before landing on the roof and crushing me in. I had heard about your life flashing before you and for me this was a sign that I wasn't going to die but live because the flash movie that played out before me had me still hosting a talk show. And I knew then that I would survive this, because I knew that talk shows in heaven could only be hosted by Him or Oprah. So I closed my eyes and waited for whatever was next.

When the car finally landed it took me a moment to understand where I was, but again "the voice" reassured me.

"Hold on. Help is on the way." At this point, I looked over in the passenger's seat hoping for Tess or Monica from the CBS television show, *Touched by an Angel*. Either would do as long as it wasn't Andrew, the angel of death.

"Hold on and know that I wouldn't let anything happen to you. But you can help yourself, crawl on the roof of the car and make your way to the back seat."

I did as I was told and by the time "help" arrived I was trying to escape the car before anything could happen. As I tried to gain enough composure to get out, I saw the relieved faces of EMT and other concerned witnesses. As I was removed from the car I heard "the voice" say again, "Never leave you, nor forsake you."

I was laid on the ground hurting. Everyone told me that I was really lucky—no make that blessed—to even be alive, confessing that they expected a corpse. I whispered a quick prayer and thanks. As I look back, grace, mercy, and protection were my three angels as I was virtually unscathed, and I was glad that God wasn't just somewhere but that He was right there.

 # *The Breaking of Day*

Then your light shall break forth like the morning.
Your healing shall spring forth speedily; And your
righteousness shall go before you; The glory of the
Lord shall be your rear guard. Then you shall call, and
the Lord will answer; You shall cry,
and He will say, "Here I am."
Isaiah 58: 8-9 (KJV)

I spent the past ten years of my life in the dark. The funny thing is, I didn't even know it! I was walking around playing the role of "mommy," "wife," "career woman," "counselor/advisor," "fly girl," etc. I really thought I had it goin' on!

How could I not when I had the man of my dreams, a beautiful daughter and a hotshot job in my career field. I was also in great physical shape — eating healthy, exercising every day and loving it!

But wait a minute! If I really had it this good, why was I mad all the time? Why was I staying up late at night and drinking myself to sleep? Why was my husband gone more than he was home? And why did I hate my 'hotshot' job? I didn't like myself much either. I was keeping up appearances in public while falling completely apart in private.

Little did I know then, these were all God's wake-up calls. He was desperately trying to get my attention but I wasn't listening.

Sure, I was going to church on Sunday, but you've heard the saying, "Go to church on Sunday...and raise hell the rest of the week." That was me! My soul and my spirit were in total darkness. I had no clear direction or any sense of who I was.

Added to this mess of a life was the fact that I was sick. Diagnosis: Hyperthyroid and congestive heart failure. It took its toll on my relationship with my daughter, almost cost me my job and more importantly, it almost took my life. More wake-up calls.

It took all of this, plus being homeless for a short period of time to finally get my attention. One afternoon, I went to the sanctuary of my church, broke down and prayed. I asked God for direction, even if it meant trying to save my marriage, I would submit. I asked Him to remove the darkness from my spirit and invited Him to come in and let His light shine through me.

It was at that point I realized when you have nothing else, you have faith. Faith becomes more valuable to you than all the money in the world. The following Sunday, while sitting in church, one of our associate ministers delivered a message about being in the pit and how God will help you get out if you just call on Him. That was the wake-up call I responded to. I began to see the breaking of day.

Today, I am a happily divorced mother of a beautiful 12 – year-old.

0 > $66,622

by Franc Levion

Are ye not much better than they?
Matthew 6:26b (KJV)

Ever give a cashier $10 for a purchase and get back change for a $20 bill? What was your response? Recently, I faced a similar dilemma. Here is my story.

Nearly four years ago, I was appointed director of a new department in local government. Working closely with a Board of 18 elected and appointed officials, our mission was to improve interagency cooperation and reduce bureaucratic turf battles to keep children and youth from falling through the cracks of the human service system.

During my third year as director I circulated a memo raising serious questions about the policies and practices of specific agencies. To stress my commitment to my department's mission, I stated that if the Board members were unwilling to make the recommended changes to their respective agencies, then my department and the Board should be dissolved. Many Board members implicated in my criticisms were angry and offended.

My memo—by "speaking truth to power"—launched a chain of life-altering events. A few weeks later the Board held a closed session. The county manager informed me three hours later that he was transferring me to a lower level position in another department, though I could keep my salary of $66,622. I was not impressed. I asked him why I was being demoted. He matter-of-factly replied, "I don't have a problem with your performance. Your evaluations exceed expectations. Franc, they're politicians." He encouraged me to consider his offer and to feel free to present a counter-offer. Taking his advice seriously, the following week I presented him with my counter-proposal, to work as a clinical social worker in the Mental Health Department. If I was to be transferred, I wanted a placement where I could make the greatest impact. Having observed the gaps in the system of care the past three years, I knew there was a critical shortage of psychotherapists serving children in our community. When my counter-offer was rejected, I chose to resign rather than accept their offer to work as an overpaid paper-shuffler.

I had always vowed never to quit my job without having another. At the time, one of my colleagues had encouraged me to accept the transfer until I found a suitable position. But I told him, "Since my rational mind never considered accepting that job, I know my spiritual mind is in total control."

In the 6th Chapter of Matthew, Jesus told the disciples, "Do not be anxious about your life, what you shall eat or what you shall drink, nor about your body, what you shall put on. Look at the birds of the air: they neither sow nor reap nor gather into barns, yet your heavenly Father feeds them. Consider the lilies of the field how they grow; they neither toil nor spin. Are you not of more value than they?"

These past 10 months, God has literally taken care of me while my life seemingly fell apart. I am still unemployed and my former employer successfully appealed my right to receive unemployment benefits. Besides my harrowing employment experience, I had surgery to rule out breast cancer, I lost my beloved grandfather and stepfather, and my minister-husband abandoned me and our two-year marriage. It is truly by God's grace that I got over. My late grandfather, a Baptist minister, taught me as a little girl to put my confidence in God, not man (Psalm 118:8). Before this experience, I thought I'd fully embraced His teaching. But now I see I really believed other people needed God more than I, because I could take care of myself. Finally, I was forced to accept my dependence on God's grace. He has done a better job than I ever have.

As tears of praise streamed down my cheeks one Saturday morning, I thanked God for peace of mind and never being hungry, homeless, cold, hot, or harassed by creditors throughout this ordeal. I often think of the lyrics from a song in *The New National Baptist Hymnal*. "He is with me in my trials, Best of friends of all is He; I can always count on Jesus, Can He always count on me?" I believe God expected me to count on Him instead of allowing man to mistreat me for "speaking the truth." I hope He is satisfied with me.

Everyday Miracles
by Valerie E. Cousin

Lord, is it you? Tell me to come on water.
Matthew 14:28 (NIV)

Like Peter, we often want to know if it is the voice of Jesus calling us to change jobs; to fellowship with a particular congregation; to make decisions one way or the other. However, when Jesus speaks to us, through the divine guidance of the Holy Spirit, we often respond with "Lord, is it you?" Sometimes, we may ask for a sign like: "If this is the right job for me, let them make me an offer!" or "If this is the right spouse, let him propose to me." If responses to our questions are favorable, then we regard the response as the voice of God. However, if we don't receive a response or if we receive an unfavorable response, we are more inclined to continue seeking God's face until we receive a favorable response.

Now when Peter heard Jesus reply favorably, he got out of the boat and began to walk on water toward Jesus. But when he saw the wind, he became afraid, took his eyes off Jesus and began to sink.

When I was job-hunting in the Spring of 1997, I was offered three positions. I said, "Lord, if it's you, they'll make me an offer." The problem is that I received offers for two of the three positions for which I had applied. One position was near home and the other position was located in New York City. The one near home offered a salary that was $15,000 less than my current salary. The other position offered several thousand dollars more than my current position. So, I had a problem.

Instead of revisiting my petition to God which was "Lord, please make a way for me to work near home so I can spend more time with my children," I blindly accepted the position that offered more money. To my dismay, however, the position turned out to be nothing of what I expected and the eight-month experience was a nightmare. I began sending out resumes after one month on the job!

Jesus said to Peter, "You of little faith, why did you doubt. And when they climbed into the boat, the wind died down and those who were in the boat worshipped him saying, Truly, you are the Son of God."

I, like Peter had to reach rock bottom, sinking in the daily drama that continued to unfold, before I realized I had to trust God to take control of my situation. I began to pray and ask God to deliver me. God revealed to me, through the Holy Spirit, that if I am to be a victor in this situation, I had to obey His word. I must begin "doing all things as unto the Lord."

Although I did not understand this at first, the scripture began to come alive each day as I meditated upon it. The Spirit spoke into my spirit: when you are living for me, you need to make sure that your home life, your work ethic, your conduct, your spiritual being reflect my love, grace and mercy... Do all things, Valerie, as if you were doing them for me. That was deep!

After being in prayer for quite some time (and I really mean some time!), I began to have a *change* in attitude. I began to act like a servant of God [not a manservant!] *even* when I didn't feel like it.

The results? After working six-months in a hostile environment, I received an *excellent* rating on my probationary evaluation and a hope that all would be all right! This too was my ticket to look for a new job; for you see, you can't get a good reference from a supervisor you are not getting along with.

As I reflected on this experience, I was reminded of that scripture in the book of James [paraphrased] *faith without works is dead, being alone.* So after the prayer, after the change in attitude, after the resume mailing, I began to sit back and wait for my miracle! Two months into the process, I was called to interview for a position for which I had not applied. I applied for a Director of Grants position, but was asked to interview for a Controller position. Turns out the current Controller was sitting on the search committee for the Director of Grants position, saw my resume and thought I would better serve the institution as the Controller instead of the Director of Grants. After attending a series of interviews, I was offered the position with a whopping $20,000 increase in salary!

Like Peter's rescue from the raging sea, my rescue from an ill-fitted position is a miracle that happens every day for those who believe in the power of God and in the power of His Might!

I was so pleased with God moving in my life at just the right time (not in my time, but His!), that I wanted to just scream when I received the offer! In fact, I just held the phone with the biggest smile on my face while the offer was being made. I then hung up the phone and just leaped for joy as I celebrated yet another miracle of God!

Afterwards, I began to pray and to thank God for the "bad" experience and for allowing me to persevere until the end.

If I had not accepted the Assistant Director of Grants position—the bad experience—I would not have been qualified to apply for the Director of Grants position at the other institution. It was through that application that God was able to use someone on that committee to elevate me to my current position. So you see, I had to go through. It was in the cards. God said in Romans 8:28 He will work all things to the good of those who love Him and are called according to His purpose.

Faith-Building Through Prayer
by Patricia A. Mathis

Be still, and know that I am God: I will be exalted among the heathen, I will be exalted in the earth.
Psalm 46:10 (KJV)

The summer of 1966 proved to be a faith-building year for me. My 78-year-old grandfather had suffered a stroke, and his life lay in the balance. My entire family was in a state of shock and upset. The thought of losing the patriarch of our family was overwhelming.

I remember so well the first evening grandpa spent in the hospital. It was doubtful that he would last the night. The doctors had told us to prepare for the worse. Even if he lived, he would be incapacitated for the rest of his life. I went to bed that evening, but couldn't sleep. I was totally distraught, and felt hopeless. As I sobbed uncontrollably I got on my knees and pleaded with our Father to let my grandpa live. After a while, a sense of peace surrounded me. It was the presence of the Holy Spirit that was there, in my bedroom, comforting me. I knew without a doubt that my grandfather would be all right.

I heard my mother in the kitchen preparing breakfast. To my amazement, it was morning! Without realizing it, I had been in prayer all night long. Through this experience, I learned at an early age, that there is tremendous power in prayer, and that when we earnestly pray things do change. Over the years I have drawn on this experience to steady and hold on to my faith, and to remain hopeful. I know that I can go through anything because my Father handles everything. I just need to get out of the way and let Him do that.

The Lord allowed my grandfather to live five years after his stroke. To the surprise of his doctors he talked and walked and even built a fireplace in my mother's basement after his illness. Praise be to God for providing situations and opportunities for us to learn how to depend on Him and to use His marvelous gift of prayer.

Five Generations of Faith

And I will establish My covenant between Me and you and your descendants after you in their generations, for an everlasting covenant, to be God to you and your descendants after you.
Genesis 17:7 (NKJV)

Our family was atypical—grandparents and extended family numbering twelve. The family was stable, close and rooted in the African Methodist Episcopal Church. Because of the racism in our society, our socialization took place in the church. We had mentors and role models within the church family. Growing up in the inner city, we were fortunate in that we did not have to deal with the ills in our current society, namely: drugs, alcohol abuse, gangs, pornography, life threatening diseases, lottery, riverboats, etc. Everyone I knew had a healthy work ethic and did not believe the government should or would provide for their needs.

Education was expected. Good grades in school were not only asked for, but demanded by family and the larger society. Our role models were our parents, neighbors, Sunday School teachers, and most of all the African Methodist Episcopal ministers. They provided structure and a sense of order to our lives. They presented hope for the future and we listened and learned from them. They were looked up to because of their exemplary lifestyles.

I married a Christian man during my early adult years; raised two boys the only way I knew how—in the church. I completed my education and through the years remained in the same church of my childhood and worked in this church in many capacities. As a reward, the Lord has provided me all the joy and comforts I could ever need or want. My children and grandchildren are whole, God-fearing human beings. They are happy, healthy and best of all, working in the African Methodist Episcopal Church. We have always put God first in the practical as well as the spiritual issues of our lives. The role of matriarch fits me well. I owe it all to the Lord Jesus Christ who guides me daily through life. Like Paul, "my determination is to be utmost for His Highest."

 In His Care

God cares for you, so turn all your worries over to him.
1 Peter 5:7 (CEV)

God's blessed spirit and presence has guided, protected, and sustained me all the years of my life. I will share only two incidents at this time.

During my teen years and early adulthood, my family lived in a neighborhood where we would go to the 63rd Street shopping area around Halsted in Chicago. To get there, we went through two underpasses—the one on State Street, which was about a block long and the one on 63rd Street was about two or three blocks.

On my way home one afternoon, under the long underpass, I saw a menacing figure approach me. There was no way to escape. Then I felt God's divine presence behind me.

Evidently the male figure, which had been approaching me, saw the presence too. All of a sudden, he turned around and fled. I continued on. When I got to the end of the underpass, no one was there.

On another occasion as an adult I faced a week where I had little ready cash. On this particular day I was on my way to work with just enough carfare to get there. I had planned to try to borrow some money for carfare home.

Just as I approached the bus stop, three greenbacks came blowing down the street—a five-dollar bill and two one-dollar bills. Of course with that seven dollars my immediate financial needs—through prayer and supplication—were taken care of for the rest of the week.

When I hear folk saying to me "Oh, you got money," little do they realize is that I "have God" and He supplies and cares. And I thank and praise His name daily.

So I just smile at them and go on, for I am in His care.

For a Closer Walk with God

by Jurlene Glover

Vindicate me, O LORD, For I have walked in my integrity. I have also trusted in the LORD; I shall not slip. Examine me, O LORD, and prove me; Try my mind and my heart. For Your lovingkindness is before my eyes, And I have walked in Your truth.
Psalm 26:1-3 (NKJV)

My husband got a tiny sore on his leg that turned into a large, excruciating sore. None of the doctors in our small town were able to stop the pain or heal the leg. Sometimes I look back on my life three years ago and I can't help but be grateful to God for faithfulness. He promised He would never leave us and I believe that's what kept me from giving up.

Finally, my husband was sent to Toledo, Ohio for three operations. God blessed me to have friends to give me a helping hand when needed. They would drive me over to Toledo to the hospital and nursing home. I decided one weekend to drive myself to the nursing home and got lost on the way. While traveling, I put my trust in God. I felt Him by my side. I sang Christian songs, prayed and recited scripture when I was lost on the Interstate. I had never driven on the Interstate in a large city before, but I put my trust in God. I knew He was with me every step of the way.

I visited my husband often, took him treats, prayed with him and did all I could to keep his spirits up. His leg did finally heal, but he was unable to stand or sit up in a wheelchair. This was disappointing as he had been able to walk after his first operation. He was transferred to a nursing home in our small town for rehabilitation therapy. After three months, his therapy was finished and God saw fit for me to take him home. He was able to walk with a walker and a gait belt. I retired from my job to take care of him. It was quite a job, but God was with me every step of the way. The strength that it took to take care of him had to come only from God. We had a wonderful time at first, but as time went on, various parts of his body wore out and life became difficult. Sometimes I was only able to sleep for three hours, but God gave me the strength to get up and function as if I had slept for eight hours.

After fourteen months of living at home, one Sunday I had to send him to the hospital for observation. He was readmitted to the nursing home where I visited him twice a day. Ten days later, he had a heart attack and other complications. It was difficult to pick up the pieces after being married for 37 years. At first, I thought I couldn't make it, but I reached out to my Lord and he dulled the pain. After my beloved husband's death I realized that all of the tribulations that I had experienced were fulfilling my mission for a closer walk with God.

Renewed Faith
by Irma M. Williams

Restore us to yourself, O Lord , that we may return;
renew our days as of old
Lamentations 5:21 (NIV)

I gave my son permission to travel from Flint to Idlewild, Michigan with a co-worker and her two sons for one week. They left on a Sunday afternoon in August 1955. On Tuesday afternoon he drowned in the lake. His body was recovered on Wednesday morning. I was notified of this by the A.M.E. Pastor.

For a short period of time I lost my faith in God. With the help of my mother and the support of family and friends as well as constant prayer, I realized that I had to help myself with God's help and guidance.

I made a decision to relocate to Detroit where the home office of my employer was located. I was welcomed with open arms and united with a church in which I became active. My new friends helped me get through my ordeal. In addition to losing my son, his father had died of lung cancer. In Detroit I met my present husband, who ironically had the same last name as my deceased husband. God answered my prayers by giving me another son and now I have a lovely family including three beautiful grandchildren. Thanks be to God for His mercy.

Stepping Out on Faith
by Trevy A. McDonald

God is the one who began this good work in
you, and I am certain that he won't stop before it is
complete on the day that Christ Jesus returns.
Philippians 1:6 (CEV)

God speaks to all of us, but sometimes we are too busy caught up in life to listen and obey His voice. Sometimes we get the same message repeatedly from a variety of sources, only instead of looking to God, we allow fear to overtake faith. Instead of looking at our own accomplishments and at how God has brought us through life, we think of our inexperience and insecurities and use them to keep us from where God wants us to be.

In 1995 I found myself armed with a Ph.D. at age 25 but unemployed. The previous academic year I chose to focus on completing my dissertation rather than the time-consuming job search. I had set a goal for myself and attained that goal. I felt that with all of the colleges and universities across the nation I would surely find a position somewhere. Unfortunately that didn't happen right away.

For the first time in my life since I was four years old, Labor Day came and I was not on my way back to school. I refused to become depressed about my situation and asked myself, "What can you do now to make yourself more marketable?" While actively engaged in a job search, three book projects were born. Two were scholarly anthologies, which grew out of conference panels. The other was a novel that just popped into my head one day. Miraculously, everything fell into place for me to get the novel started.

I had been home visiting my parents for the Christmas holidays when the idea to write a novel set in. After raiding my father's collection, I borrowed a book titled *The Weekend Novelist* and returned to North Carolina where I would soon begin teaching college. Upon my arrival I laughed at the weatherman's forecast of snow. In the six years I had lived in the state, the only snow we had received melted before it ever hit the ground. Besides, for someone who had been raised in Chicago and attended college in central Wisconsin where the harsh wind and cold air caused icicles to form on my eyelashes most winter days as I walked to class, six inches of snow was nothing.

But six inches of snow in North Carolina was something. It was something big. It was six inches of snow, followed by two inches of ice, topped off by two more inches of snow, which kept me in for a week. It was then that I used *The Weekend Novelist* to develop my characters. This was significant because once I started teaching, finding the time to write was difficult. I spent most of my year teaching and searching for publishers for the scholarly books so that I could build my tenure file, and the summers in Chicago writing my first novel.

Eighteen months later, the novel was complete, and it held residence underneath my bed for a year. In the process of writing it, I formed a partnership with another writer who convinced me that we could start our own company and publish our books. When I finished the novel, my writing partner had a full plate and was unable to devote the time to starting a company and finishing her book. I still wanted to take on the challenge of publishing a novel, but truthfully I was afraid. After combing through *The Writer's Market* I learned that the major publishing houses did not accept unagented manuscripts. I queried some smaller houses, but found none interested in my manuscript. Many of them faced the challenge of receiving thousands of manuscripts annually, to only be able to publish ten or fewer titles.

Once again the idea of self-publishing the book popped into my mind. I already had the name for my publishing company. I knew who I had planned to contact for reviews. But I was still afraid. Though I had seen several authors do it successfully, I came up with a host of excuses as to why I couldn't do it. I had a full-time job and didn't have the time to devote to it, I had some health challenges, I didn't have a degree or background in business. One Sunday I took my concerns to the altar. While I didn't feel led one way or another that day, I was pleasantly surprised by an e-mail message from my friend Mark Orbe the next day.

Mark had attended church the same day I prayed for direction. While in praise and worship, Mark said God spoke to him and told him to deliver this message, "He who put a good work in you will be faithful to complete it." That was my answer and it was loud and clear. But the idea of publishing still seemed overwhelming.

Over the next few months I continued my research, developed a marketing plan and talked to a friend of a friend who had embarked on the same journey a year earlier. I also reached out to other African-American authors who were "self-published." From the sharing of their experiences, I got the inspiration I needed to move forward. Once I mapped out everything I needed to do to publish the book under the newly formed company, it only took a week for me to get everything I needed in place to send the book to the printer.

I remember how I felt when I stepped out on faith. I was comfortable, confident and at peace with myself, because I knew God was guiding each of my steps. I didn't know everything, but over and over people who could help me were put into my path and gladly offered their assistance.

Six weeks after I made the decision and stepped forward, I picked up 2,000 copies of my first novel in preparation for a series of release parties. Two weeks later, the novel was available across the United States, in Canada, in the Caribbean and in England. While the journey hasn't always been easy, it has been a true exercise in faith for me. There have been times when I've been presented with opportunities and didn't know how I would make them happen. But as I knew God was guiding my steps in the beginning, I continued to put my trust in Him. "God, you've given me this opportunity, now I trust You to work out the details," became my motto.

I learned that in order for me to step out on faith I had to leave my comfort zone and begin my journey in the right direction, which required courage. I had to gain the courage to pursue my dreams, the courage to face the unfamiliar and most of all, the courage to receive the abundant blessings.

Stepping out on faith is different from taking a risk, a term often used in business. When you take a risk, you approach it believing the outcome may be favorable or unfavorable. When you step out on faith, you are mindful of God's wisdom and guidance. And with God leading you, and even carrying you at times, how could you not be successful?

Hope

Megan's Gifts
Our Angel of
Unity and Strength
by DeAnne Winey-Ward

I have given them the glory that you gave me, that they
may be one as we are one: I in them and you in me.
May they be brought to complete unity to let the world
know that you sent me and have loved them even as
you have loved me.
John 17:22-23 (NIV)

Her life, in my own eyes began long before she was conceived, years before I even met her father. I always knew she would be special and that she would come to make a difference. Only I didn't realize what an impact she would make in such a short time period. Megan Alise was the name I chose for her when I was only in eighth grade.

When my husband of seven months and companion of seven years and I learned in early June that we would be parents on January 1, 2003, we were elated. A new year, a new baby, and new hope for the future. Most family members and friends thought from the ultrasound pictures at three months gestation that Megan would be a boy. The ultrasound tech nor the doctors said or thought she would be a boy. Her dad thought she was a boy, yet I anxiously awaited the arrival of our daughter. Megan Alise will be her name I told my husband, Jason. Unbeknownst to us, Megan would make her arrival and mark on this world sooner than we expected.

This couldn't be. On August 15 as I took a bath, my
membrane ruptured (water broke). I was only 20 weeks
pregnant. My husband called the doctor and I was
immediately rushed to the hospital for an undetermined
length of stay. My doctor informed me that I would not be
going home until I had my baby. The medical goal was to
not have contractions or infection, to accumulate more
amniotic fluid, and hold the baby in the womb as long as
my body would allow. Our short-term goal was 24 weeks,
at which time I would receive steroid shots to help the
baby's lungs develop. The doctors weren't hopeful that my
child would make it through the next four weeks. The on-
call physician said the most likely outcome was that I would
develop and infection and deliver the baby within the next
three days. My regular OB/GYN of seven years remained
optimistic and willing to go the extra mile to ensure that I
had the best medical care. The first Perinatologist informed
us that my amniotic fluid level was below a five, almost
near nothing. The second Perinatologist said bluntly that
even if I held the baby until thirty-weeks that she would not
make it. The last Perinatologist reviewed all the facts of the
situation, but left me with hope and the optimistic view to
keep fighting to give my baby the best chance possible
without any regrets of the "what if?" The last
Perinatologist, the Neonatologist, and my OB/GYN were a
wonderful team and left me with the only thing I had to
keep going — "hope."

Most of my family members live in a city three hours away,
but they came the distance to rally around and support
Jason and I. My brother, whom I hadn't spoken to in three
years, traveled twelve hours from North Carolina. My
parents, who have been married for 31 years, rekindled their
love for each other and once again grew close and giggled in
each other's presence like young teenage lovers. Megan's
God-mother's support was endless. She emptied my bed

pans, gave sponge baths, cried with me, kissed my stomach every time she left and never missed one day from visiting me while in the hospital.

Unfortunately, I went into labor a day short of 24 weeks gestation. My doctor tried to stop the labor, but was unsuccessful with medications. I delivered by Caesarian Section, a one pound, one ounce baby girl named, Megan Alise Ward, on September 9, 2002. The neonatal doctors were hopeful that Megan would live, but as the night went on, her heart rate dropped. Megan's lungs were underdeveloped and she experienced some respiratory failure. Megan passed away in my arms around 2:00 a.m. on September 10 — a week after my 31st birthday.

She was amazing and lived a lifetime within seven hours. She gave our family so much and I am so proud of her. She changed the lives of many, even some of the hospital staff. Everyone, from hospital RNs, to dietary, to housekeeping, to the social services department, was saddened by her early passing. It was all so obvious by their presence at her funeral services. My daughter's neonatal specialist called and asked to have lunch a few weeks after her passing. How many doctors you just meet call you after the fact and say let's have lunch, I care? Where my daughter's mission ended, mine had just begun.

In Megan's funeral service programs I wrote the following:

She united family and friends — "togetherness." She healed broken relationships.

She enriched and heightened the love between her parents.

She increased the faith level of many people. She confirmed for us what we already know: God is an awesome God.

God is love. She introduced new friends into our lives who we were able to share our faith in God.

She allowed us the opportunity to share with people what faith in God can do—the Lord is full of miracles and blessings. Look to the Lord always, even in the darkest hours and He will fill your spirit with a sense of peace.

She showed us that having or acquiring "stuff" in life is not important, but genuinely caring and supportive family and friends are priceless.

The victory is ours and we claim it in Jesus' name. Jason and I will complete our mission here on earth and after, we will be joined again with our Angel to rejoice in eternal life with our Lord and Savior Jesus Christ.

Premature Rupture of Membranes or PROM as it is called occurs during pregnancy when the sac containing the developing baby and the amniotic fluid bursts or develops a hole prior to the start of labor. The causes of PROM haven't been clearly identified although some risk factors, procedures and conditions are related to PROM. There are two types of PROM. One occurs at a point in pregnancy before normal labor and delivery should take place. This is called preterm PROM. The other type of PROM occurs between 36-40 weeks of pregnancy.

PROM occurs in about 10 percent of all pregnancies. Only about 20 percent of these cases are preterm PROM. Preterm PROM is responsible for about 34 percent of all premature births (*Gale Encyclopedia of Medicine*. Gale Research, 1999). In 1988, President Ronald Reagan proclaimed October as Pregnancy and Infant Loss Awareness Month throughout the United States. October 15 is the day of candle lighting celebration by the Share Organization. Awareness is important, as is dedicating a specific time of year to educate others and memorialize our loved ones who have passed away. Pregnancy and infant losses occur more often than the average person realizes. Consider the following: Each year, hundreds of thousands of families are faced with the tragedy of pregnancy and infant loss. According to 1999 Centers of Disease Control statistics, only 62 percent of all pregnancies result in live births.

Parents whose lives are touched by the tragic death of a baby through miscarriage, stillbirth or newborn death are misunderstood by many who have not experienced such a loss. People outside of the immediate family circle tend to feel that if a child was lost due to miscarriage, or if a child did not come home to live with the family, that the loss is a minor, unfortunate event. But from the moment parents learn they are expecting, they make an investment in their unborn child, sometimes this emotional investment is made prior to conception. Like parents of living children, these parents have hopes, dreams, anticipation and most of all, love for the unborn child. Education and awareness are important in understanding the medical aspects of PROM as well as the emotional devastation of the families who experience such a tragedy.

For more information on Premature Rupture of Membrane or Pregnancy & Infant Loss Support visit
www.kanalen.org/prom
www.nationalshareoffice.com,
www.pregnancyandinfantloss.com

A Ram in the Bush
by Annie Marie Ford

Abraham looked up and saw a ram caught by its horns
in the bushes. So he took the ram and sacrificed it in
place of his son. Abraham named that place "The
LORD Will Provide." And even now people say, "On
the mountain of the LORD it will be provided."
Genesis 22:13-14 (CEV)

After attending the Women's Leadership Conference in Detroit in 1999 and hearing the dynamic woman speakers, our Missionary Society selected a speaker for our day. The preparations were done, invitations mailed and programs were printed.

On the morning of the program, at 7:30 a.m., my telephone rang. It was our speaker for the day who informed me that she was ill and unable to speak for us. As this was my first time serving as President of the Society and Program Co-Coordinator, I was at a loss of what I should do. I was not afraid, because I had confidence that my God would provide a replacement speaker for us.

I immediately telephoned one of my best friends, who is also a member of my church, and informed her of the situation. She gave me the name and telephone number of a potential speaker. I called this person, introduced myself and told her of our dilemma.

She informed me that she was normally not home at that time as she is usually at Sunday School and that I was fortunate to catch her at home. She graciously accepted my invitation to come as our replacement speaker upon approval of release time from her pastor.

Her pastor approved her coming to our rescue and she was a fantastic speaker. Our society enjoyed her message immensely. Our *Ram in the Bush* speaker was given an opportunity to prepare a message especially for our society and invited back to speak at our 2001 Annual Missionary Day.

 *Love Never Fails*
by Michele Rene Matthews

Behold, I set before you this day a blessing and a curse;
A blessing if ye obey the commandments of the Lord
your God, which I command you this day And a curse,
if ye will not obey the commandments of the Lord your
God, but turn aside out of the way which I command
you this day, to go after other gods, which ye have not
known.
Deuteronomy 11:26-28 (KJV)

The most difficult aspect of my decision to leave my marriage was the fact that I knew I was being disobedient to God; that I was acting contrarily to His word. 1 Corinthians 7:10 clearly states that a wife shall not depart from her husband. During that time I was sad and frustrated and I convinced myself that I knew what was best for me and I resolved to allow God to deal with me because of my disobedience. I was acting under the assumption that obedience was a choice and I chose to ask for forgiveness for leaving rather than for permission to leave. Acts 5:29 states that we must obey God rather than man (or ourselves). Clearly obedience is not a choice.

I was disappointed with my marriage and I saw no way out except the front door. During the two-year separation my emotions ranged from sadness to bitterness. I got involved in situations that can only be described as self-destructive. I blamed myself and I blamed my husband and in the end I truly believed that love did not even exist and if it did, I wouldn't recognize it if it wore a nametag. I was a mess.

I enjoy a successful career in government contracting; I've written one novel and have published a few short essays. I am a mother to two healthy, intelligent, well-adjusted children. For real—I have it going on. Yet, for an entire year my constant prayer was, "Lord, teach me how to love."

God works in mysterious ways. It is not just a cliché. I can't even pinpoint how it happened. The last thing I remember is sitting on my bed and having a conversation with God. I was having this particular conversation with the Lord because so many people around me were suggesting that maybe I still had feelings for my ex and that it wasn't unreasonable for us to get back together. That was the furthest thing from my mind, but there was some reason why so many people were coming to me with the same message. I was talking to God about my ex-husband and here's what I said: "Lord, you know how I feel. I do not want that man. But if that's what you want for me then you'll have to do it because I don't want him. What I do want is to be obedient to you, Lord. But you'll have to do it." At that moment, I gave it all to God. I was willing to put aside my feelings and what I wanted in order to be obedient. It wasn't until I surrendered the situation to God that he took control. I believe that God looks at us sometimes and says, "Look, either you're gonna do it, or I'm gonna do it --but we're both not gonna do it."

God did it. I don't know how but God allowed me to see my ex-husband through His eyes. God showed me how to love my ex-husband again through obedience to Him. We are on the road to reconciliation because God is faithful and His word is true.

Praying with Your Children
by Norma J. Gibbs

Again I say unto you, That if two of you shall agree on earth as touching any thing that they shall ask, it shall be done for them of my Father which is in heaven.
Matthew 18:19 (KJV)

One morning when my youngest child was only four years old my husband was told that he had lung cancer. My other children were grown and living on their own so my youngest child and I were the only family members present to offer support. My husband's prognosis was so serious that we were told he only had a few months to live. While surgery could keep him alive a little longer, my husband had given up hope and said he was going to die.

The next morning it was so strong in my heart to agree with someone in prayer that he would live. The only person around was my four-year-old daughter. I asked her, "Do you believe that God can heal Daddy and make him well?" She looked at me with her big brown eyes and said, "Yes

Mommy." So we prayed for my husband to receive the healing that Jesus died for. I said by his stripes we were healed. I spoke out in the name of Jesus, receive your healing.

In the next moment, Robin said her Daddy was not going to die. That night I asked God to please let my husband live to see my four-year-old daughter to adulthood. He lived until she was about 22 years old.

God does answer prayer.

 Between the Cracks

The Lord is good to those whose hope is in him,
to the one who seeks him; it is good to wait quietly
for the salvation of the Lord.
Lamentations 3:25-26 (NIV)

"Today is the beginning of the rest of my life." That was my daily motto as I began my walk in the surf along the shores of the Atlantic Ocean. That walk was a part in my quest for a long forgotten emotion, which had escaped me for too many years. This was not a forgotten emotion, but a feeling lost for too many years—peace of mind. I was not even aware when I lost this feeling because it was such a natural feeling, a warm gift from my loving and protective parents and sisters and brothers. Even though the journey through my childhood often felt like I was a caterpillar in a cocoon— tightly enfolded and held close, the closeness was always warm and endearing. That cocoon was never so tight as to bruise or cause pain, but it created a sense of well-being, a closeness of security and overflowing with love. That family closeness was gentile and directed.

As I would lie motionless in the surf as the salt water slowly ebbed its way over my body, I began to think about my father, Mr. William P., who was always referred to as Mr. P. by the white folks who often asked permission to sit on our front porch in the early evening and talk to Daddy. They could not even walk on <u>his</u> sidewalk without his permission; since we had the only sidewalk on McLeod Street, which was named in honor of Dr. Mary McLeod Bethune who founded Bethune-Cookman College. These white men were not his friends, but those who possibly served him in the McFarland Furniture Store or Yowell-Drew Ivey Department Store and liked to discuss his philosophy of life or politics. These stores had the better quality of furniture and clothing. Mr. P. bought nothing that was what he would consider cheap, whether clothes or furniture for his family.

A common sight was to see the white insurance men who walked the streets in Midway to collect for the twenty-five cents weekly insurance policy from the black policyholders. They would approach Mr. P's yard, move to the street, pass in front of his property, then return to the yards of the neighbors, continuing on their debit. Midway, a section of the black community where the black college was located was where our family physician, Dr. Stocking, lived. Dr. Slack, the community pharmacist and the Ritz Theatre were all in this area, which was known as the better part of town for black families.

The phrase "Between the Rocks" relates to a remembrance that sends a warm glow of memory of my early childhood. I was a real Tomboy because I was the fifth child in a family

of six siblings—four brothers and one older sister who was
the second born. I had a younger brother, William III, who
was five years my junior. I was a real Tomboy at age ten. My
father would take the two of us to the Tomoka, where the
Halifax River trickled through boulder-like rocks down to
the Atlantic Ocean. He would allow my brother Bill and me
to walk the rocks to the other side. My dad would warn us
to be careful, because the rocks were covered with algae and
one could slide from the rocks into the stream with a slight
shift of one's balance. My father would encourage us to get
back upon the rocks and try again. His encouraging words
were "Don't give up. Keep trying. You'll get the hang of
how to stay on top." Those words still ring in my heart.

Today is the beginning of the rest of my life! "Don't give up.
Keep trying. You'll get the hang of how to stay on top.
You're a big boy! You're a big girl!" Actually, those words
appeared before me mentally as I stood watching the
sailboats go by as they floated down the Halifax River past
the County Courthouse Annex on the beautiful seaside. This
was the eighth and last post-divorce suit. I stood between
the rocks and looked up towards the slimy rocks.

Anger had caused my ex-husband to begin a journey of
deep revenge against me because I divorced him. He took
all of the money from our joint bank account, then sued me
eight times including for a Cosco stool which I had
purchased with *S & H Gold Stamps*. The final blow was
when he was awarded custody of my thirteen-year-old son.
He won every time. He had money, I had none. He had a
lawyer and I didn't . Wounded and bruised, I left the state,
taking everything I owned, including a four-bedroom ranch
style home with a three-car garage, which sat on an acre of
land. A furniture moving company stuck my belongings on
the back of a truck bound for the big city out of the state.
The total cost of the move was $172.00 and a plane ticket.

Four years later, my son ran away and came to where I was hard at work on my advanced degree.

Usually, when there is a severe hurt, a person will turn to what they know in order to succeed. I went back to school. I would leave work in the downtown area of the city, catch a bus and travel twenty-eight miles to a small suburb where there was an off-campus site for a major university to begin my doctoral studies. If my class ended at 10:30 p.m., my advisor could drop me off at the airport in that area and I would catch the last bus back to the city, then go to work the next morning. If the class went over time by ten minutes, the bus would have left. I then would have to wait two hours for a late flight to come in so that I could share a taxicab going back into the city. My limited budget would only allow a single cab ride. This was my focus for two years.

When I completed my preliminary examinations, I had to move to the campus in the mountains, which was a five-hour drive from the city. I had no car when I moved to the city because someone had put sugar in my gas tank, ruining the motor of my vehicle. My banker suggested that I not attempt to purchase another car because of my financial status at that time. He suggested that I use public transportation in the city. He promised to assist me in a purchase later on. I moved to the university town with an old bicycle with an old rusty basket, in which I planned to carry my books as I pedaled to classes. I obviously did not know my geography or remember my age. The university campus and community was a very beautiful, mountainous area—hardly a place conducive to a forty-year-old riding up and down the mountainside.

When the university had its annual surplus sale, some of my friends accompanied me. With their vigorous assistance, I laid claim to a 20-year-old light blue Buick with a fifty-dollar deposit from my very limited funds. I called my brother, Jr., that night and told him what I had done. I proudly informed him that the vehicle had 88,000 miles on it. He screamed and after using a few choice words, offered to send me $1,000. This was to pay down on a new automobile. I was fortunate to have siblings who always helped whomever was in school. I reminded my banker that he had said, "When you get ready I will intercede with a dealership for you to get a vehicle." He kept his word and very shortly I was driving a brand new Nissan Hatchback. That day was the beginning of the rest of my life. I was temporarily on my way back to the top of the rocks.

While I continued to work on my preliminary papers to qualify as a full-fledged doctoral student, I kept one of my consulting jobs in the city to survive. This meant that I had to travel to the city around the mountains, through heavy snow and sleet. I would leave the mountains at midnight on Thursday nights and drive alone, arriving in the city the next morning at 5:00 a.m. I usually stopped for an hour at a busy truck stop in one of the valleys going through the Shenandoah's to pray and have one of the new sausage biscuits and coffee.

My destination in the city was a high profile condominium building with 24-hour guards. This was the building, which caused former President Richard Nixon's downfall. The guards were tiny, strange looking creatures weighing less than one hundred pounds. They could scale the inner courtyard walls of that high profile security building like spiders. One had to have clearance to enter the complex.

My work began Friday morning and ended Sunday afternoon, at 3:00 p.m. I would then begin my five-hour trek back up the mountains to my temporary home to work on my dissertation.

I worked for the education department, which made all of the office materials I needed to work on my paper. I worked for the university eight hours a day beginning at 8:00 a.m. and left at 5:00 p.m. After rushing home to take a nap and eat a quick bite, I spent an hour in the gym and returned to my office at 7:00 p.m. where I wrote until 5:00 a.m. I returned home, took a quick nap, ate a light breakfast and returned to my regular job. This was my schedule for two years.

My wardrobe was very limited. My most embarrassing experience was when I was able to buy a cheap pair of shoes in the spring, discarding the shoes that I had worn all year. I wore them to work the next day. One of the female faculty members looked up and greeted me warmly stating, "Oh hello, I did not recognize you, you have on a different pair of shoes." I could only smile when I realized that she had never really looked at me, the person. I was recognized, by the familiar shoes that I wore daily. I was a non-person to her as long as I fulfilled my duties in that office. I had a master's degree and really didn't have to take this humiliation. I could leave right this minute. At that very moment, I heard a familiar voice say, "Don't give up (swallow your pride). Keep trying. You'll get the hang of how to stay on top." I grew three feet tall, nourishing my own new self-confidence. Today was the beginning of the rest of my life.

Much water has passed under the bridge since those days I walked on the algae covered rocks, avoiding falling between the cracks. Our loving God gave me an unusually loving mate. We nourish each other every minute of the day and even in our sleeping hours. We enjoy each other's presence. There are those who had hoped and predicted that it would not last. Our success lies in the fact that our heavenly father always keeps us balanced. Even when we are at risk of "falling between the cracks," He gives us balance. We are so full of God's grace that we continuously nourish those who come into our presence. We have too many spiritual children who have adopted us. My beloveds are pleased with the blessing, which God has given our children. Our son has the real father he never had. Our children are all happily married and they have given us beautiful grandchildren. Each day is the beginning of the rest of our lives in God's daily blessings and love.

 ## Lynn and the Angel
by Aj D. Jemison

Do not forget to entertain strangers, for by so doing some people have entertained angels without knowing it.
Hebrews 13:2 (NIV)

Farmer's Bank held the accounts for several members of Gloria's family. So on this particular day she couldn't help but notice the new teller behind the counter. Yet there was something very familiar about the young lady, with her dark skin, wavy, jet-black hair and beautiful smile. When Gloria got to the front of the line she asked her name. "Lynn," she replied, as they tried to remember where and how they knew each other. When Lynn indicated where she had grown up and gone to school, Gloria asked her age then realized that she was the same age as her daughter, Andrea, or "Angel" as she affectionately referred to her.

Lynn not only remembered Andrea, but recounted how they were best friends in elementary school before she moved away with her family. They lost touch and hadn't seen each other in nearly 20 years. Following their brief conversation, Gloria sought out Lynn whenever she came through the drive-thru window, until Lynn took a position at another bank location.

A year later, Lynn ran into Gloria at the grocery store and asked how to contact Andrea. Gloria got Lynn's phone number and e-mail address, promising to give them to her daughter. A couple of days later, Andrea called Lynn at work and left a message for her to check her e-mail when she got home. Lynn checked when she got home, and just as Andrea promised, there was an e-mail from her. As Lynn read the e-mail she was surprised that Andrea asked if she would do her a "favor."

The e-mail read, "Lynn, please do me a huge favor. My dad is very ill and in the hospital. His wedding anniversary is this week and I always try to give him something special and unexpected. Since you work right down the street, would you please go visit him for me? Tell him that his 'guardian angel' sent you to give him a big hug. Then tell him I sent you. That will make his day. You will be my 'stand-in angel.' His name is Anthony Lee Jackson."

Lynn thought it a bit odd that Andrea would send her to visit and hug a man she didn't even know, especially when Andrea had family living in town that could do the very thing she was being asked to do. But without another thought, Lynn e-mailed back "Sure. I'll go see your dad tomorrow."

As Lynn drove to work the next morning she had the strangest thought that Mr. Jackson's name sounded awfully familiar. "Oh my God, could it be, no that's just too much of a coincidence," she thought out loud. Yet, needless to say the thought haunted her all day.

That evening when she got home, she pulled the hospital room number off the e-mail. But she couldn't settle the uneasy thought that kept creeping into her head. She called her younger sister, Sherry, and read the e-mail to her. Lynn asked her to please go to the hospital with her for emotional support... just in case. Sherry agreed.

When Lynn and Sherry entered the hospital room that evening, she saw a man lying in the bed. She walked over to him and quietly said, "Hi, Mr, Jackson, my name is Lynn, I'm a classmate of Andrea's. She sent me here to give you a big hug for her. I'm her stand-in Angel." The man slowly smiled and sat up as she walked over to hug him. The moment they hugged, all Lynn could think was, "He's hugging me like someone who loves me." When the embrace was over, he reached up and turned on the bed light. "It was like looking in a mirror," Lynn thought.

The next thing he did caught her completely off guard. He asked, "How's your mother?" Only he called her mother by her first name. Lynn was in shock. She replied that her mother was fine. Shortly thereafter she and her sister said goodbye and left. As they walked to the elevator, her sister asked simply, "Why didn't you ask him?"

The next day, Lynn went to a card shop and bought a card. She called Mr. Jackson to inquire if it would be okay to come back for another visit. When Lynn arrived, Gloria and her granddaughter, Chanel, were there visiting. Gloria went over, hugged Lynn and said how glad she was that she had come back to visit. Lynn spent the next couple of hours talking, laughing and sharing stories about herself, in hope that Anthony Lee Jackson would realize who she was.

As it got late and Lynn prepared to leave, Gloria offered to walk her to the elevator. Along the way, Gloria told Lynn how her husband had come into her life after her previous husband was killed. She shared with her how Anthony Lee had not only been a blessing in her life for the past twenty-five years, but also the lives of her four children. She shared with her that her children didn't see him as a step-father, but just as a "Dad" and "Pops."

By that time they had reached the elevator. The elevator doors opened, but as Lynn tried to enter, she couldn't. She turned to Gloria and said, "I have to say something." Carefully choosing her words, she continued. "I hope I'm not out of line or offending you, but about three years ago I discovered that the man who raised me is not my biological dad. I think your husband is my father. I was given a name…" Before she could finish, Gloria interrupted her and said, "Oh, sweetie, that's your dad in there."

"After you left from visiting him yesterday he called me at home and just wept on the phone because he thought you still didn't know who he was." Lynn began to cry and embraced Gloria. "He has always loved you, Lynn," said Gloria. Lynn remembered the card she had in her purse, and handed it to Gloria to give it to Anthony Lee. "No," Gloria said, "You go give it to your dad and tell him you know who he really is."

Lynn walked back toward the hospital room with Gloria. Walking behind, she saw that Anthony Lee was sitting on the edge of his bed. With a puzzled expression, he looked from Gloria to Lynn. Gloria broke the silence when she stated simply, "Honey, she knows. She knows that you're her dad."

Despite his weakened physical state, Anthony Lee stood up opened his arms wide and took his daughter into his arms for the first time in over 40 years. And the tears of joy, of years lost and memory unborn began to flow from their eyes.

While they composed themselves, Gloria explained to Lynn that a young Anthony Lee had enlisted in the Army and left to go abroad without knowing that Lynn's mother was pregnant. When he returned, he found that she had gotten married to another and had a daughter. When Anthony Lee questioned the baby girl's paternity, realizing that Lynn was his daughter, he was asked by her Grandmother to never try to contact her. The grandmother told him that the child did not know and was in a loving home. Being a man of his word, he promised, and for over 40 years he never broke that promise.

Gloria told Lynn that when her husband got ill this time, she thought she might lose him and didn't think it was fair that for him not to see or hold his only biological child. She told Andrea about his past and due to Gloria coincidentally running into Lynn at the grocery store, she came up with a way to lead Lynn to Anthony Lee. Andrea thought that the least she could do for "her dad" was to give him Lynn, even if for a brief minute through a hug.

Anthony Lee asked Lynn how long she knew and how she found out. She told him about three years ago, as a result of a medical condition, she discovered that the man she knew and loved as her dad was not biologically. Even though she felt loved by her parents, there was always something missing in her life and in her heart and now she knew why.

So Lynn began the search for her biological father. The only information she had was a name, no birth date, social security number or even his last known state of residence. With nothing to go on, she continually ran into dead ends. Even those "Find a Loved One" agencies weren't able to help her. Lynn finally just had to give up, living with the sadness of probably never finding her dad, or to know if he was still alive.

Although Lynn's dad is still ill, his spirit has lifted and he is getting better, as she visits him and her newfound family almost every day. They sit holding hands, sharing details of their lives, and memories they both missed over the years. Anthony Lee is getting to know Lynn's two daughters and son, and his three great-grandsons!

 *Angels in Our Midst*
by Carolyn Burgess

For it is written: "He will command his angels concerning you to guard you carefully;
Luke 4:10 (NIV)

It had been a particularly disturbing meeting for me on this day. The inspiration of the meeting had been overshadowed by disappointing events. We went into the meeting with great hope and expectation, looking forward to our worshiping and praising the Lord together one more time, and eager to enjoy the sisterhood which these times always afford us. But this proved to be quite a different time. No matter how fervent and sincere our worship, there was a dark cloud hovering over the meeting that became more evident as the day progressed.

Finally, at the close of the day, a dear missionary sister and I stopped at the store on the way home. The day was weighing quite heavily on my mind and on my heart, and my dear missionary sister was giving encouragement to me as we rode along. At the store while walking through the aisles, we continued to discuss the events of the day. I couldn't understand the reasoning behind those things that had happened and I kept asking the question, which I had asked of God, "Why?"

We finished our shopping, had gone through the cashier's line and were about to leave. As a matter of fact the automatic doors had opened. It was then that my dear missionary sister said to me, "Someone is speaking to you."

I immediately turned to see a lady standing there with a young man. She told me her son had a special gift and wanted to do something for me. The young man stepped forward. He appeared to be around 20 years old. "Ma'am, I sense in my spirit that you are very troubled. If you would just give me about two minutes of your time, I would like to do something for you. It won't take very long."

I was curious, but reluctantly I moved closer to where they were standing. It was certainly the right thing to have done, for there in the store with people coming and going and some stopping to listen, the young man sang to me, "Battle is the Lord's." He had obviously overheard our conversation and the Lord had put it on his heart to add his ministry to that of my dear missionary sister. What a powerful moment that was. As he was singing, I could feel the burden begin to lift.

After we thanked the young man and his mother and hugged them, we proceeded out of the store to the car. Once we were in the car, my tears began to flow and it seems that the rest of my heavy burden flowed out with them. My dear missionary sister asked me if I believed in angels, and I said that I did. She said, "That's good, because God just sent one to you." Actually he had sent two, for my dear missionary sister was the first.

Whether or not you have had a similar experience, or whether or not you believe that there are guardian angels, I am a living witness that they do exist and that God sends them to us to relieve us of our pain and suffering.

 Walking with God

The LORD our God be with us, as he was with our fathers: let him not leave us, nor forsake us:
1 Kings 8:57 (KJV)

Life is filled with changes. I never imagined my life would be an uphill journey when my husband and I decided to separate. We had made plans, but I learned there was a higher power working in our lives. Like all marriages, we had problems and my husband and I came to a decision that the best way to work out our obstacles in our marriage was a trial separation. If we take the time and listen, one will find that God never lets anything come upon us without a warning.

Maybe I should start at my second birth. On January 4, 1952, I was born into this world, but on November 7, 1978, I was born again, not into the world but into Jesus Christ. At that time my whole life was centered around my husband. I couldn't imagine what my life would be like without him. I learned through my new birth that when one feels he or she can't make it in life without a certain person or thing then that person or thing has become their "GOD" and my God was my husband!

I will never forget the first Sunday in October 1978 when I came under the conviction of the Holy Spirit. I didn't understand at that time why our marriage began to suffer. Depression set in and no matter what I did to try to find joy in my life, it never came. Later that month I heard a voice say, "You didn't come this far on your own nor did your husband bring you. Before you knew your husband, I took care of you, protected you and preserved you for myself, now what have you done for me?" The following weeks after that first Sunday in October my life changed. I was caught between two worlds. I had to make a decision. On Tuesday November 7, 1978 at 9p.m., I cried out to the Lord and entrusted Him with my soul. He saved me, filled me with the Holy Spirit and I was set free. However, I became a loner in my family. No one could understand me, my husband couldn't relate to me and we began to drift apart. I have learned since then that it was the enemy fighting me through the very person who had once been my whole world. We came to the conclusion to separate for a while and if we were meant to come back together, it would work out. However, three years before we separated, the Lord showed me my husband's death. The day that God revealed this to me, my husband was coming home from work and I quickly dismissed the vision from my mind. I thought it was my imagination.

In December 1982, my three children, ages two, seven, and nine, and I began our new lives in Birmingham, Alabama, a place where we were surrounded by no one we knew. Because of the financial difficulties, I applied for Welfare and Food Stamps. My husband continued to pay the rent for our two-bedroom apartment. I didn't want to be dependent on government assistance, so I used it to my advantage. I qualified for financial aid and entered Southern Jr. College of Business. It wasn't easy. I didn't have a car, so I took the bus to school, walked to the grocery store and pushed the groceries back to the apartment in the shopping cart, and used the same tactics for laundry to the Laundromat. My two oldest kids walked to and from school regardless of the weather. During that time, I was being prepared to be on my own, getting adjusted to my husband not coming home and my children were being prepared as well. God was still in control of our lives. My husband and I had our future all planned, but on October 1, 1983 my whole world was turned upside down! At the age of 31, I became a widow, my three children now at the ages of ten, eight, and three were fatherless. My in-laws turned their backs on me, saying I was to blame for his death; if I had never moved to Birmingham, then he would have never died in that car accident. A spirit of guilt and condemnation came upon me.

My in-laws were the closest people to my husband, but they rejected me. I couldn't understand how I had been part of that family for 12 years. I learned for the first time what Jesus meant when He said, "Forgive them that trespass against you." Not only had my husband been my GOD but he was theirs also. He was the oldest of six children, and at times he was like a father to them. I can't blame them for their actions, but I knew God held me accountable for my own. I didn't have money at the time to prepare for the funeral. My father-in-law offered to help, but made sure it would be a loan. A very close friend of the family stepped in and paid for my attire to the funeral. If they could have had the funeral without me they would have, not realizing how much hurt was being inflicted on the children.

They barely spoke to me during the planning of the funeral that week. The Lord spoke to me and instructed me to include them on every aspect, because it was only a shell — the body. His spirit was gone.

The greatest healing took place when I allowed his children to be a part of their lives. To this day, they have never asked me for forgiveness, but in my heart I had to forgive.

After a feeling of guilt was placed on me I cried out to the Lord and Jesus spoke to me and reminded me of what He had shown me three years earlier. He also reminded me of the story of Lazarus. Life and death was not in my hand: St. John 11:25-26. I asked the Lord how I was going to raise three children alone. He spoke these words to me, "If you take them to church, you'll have help." St. Luke A.M.E. Church became the second parent in our lives.

My family was pressuring me to move close to them, but I had faith God would carry us through and I never wanted to let anyone become my God again. I had to trust God for myself, walk out on His promises, and believe what the Word says about "He will never leave you nor forsake you."

I cannot take credit for what God and so many people did in our lives. Jesus Christ is the answer, and to God be the glory. I won't name anyone because someone would be left out, but God put people in church, schools and the community to help guide my children.

My life took another turn in August 1994. I had two heart attacks, but that's another story of how God sheltered me and strengthened our family of four.

It wasn't easy raising three children alone, but because they were my first priority, it became a joy and a challenge. In conclusion, it's been 17 years, but through FAITH, GRACE and MERCY, and the support of the church, family and friends. My oldest son studied two years at Morehouse College in Atlanta, GA and after my illness transferred to University of Alabama to earn a BS degree in Psychology. My middle child, earned a BS degree in Nursing at Tuskegee University, and my younger child, is a senior at Tuskegee University majoring in Marketing.

There's one thing I asked the Lord to help me to accomplish and that was to leave my children a legacy of FAITH in HIM, because in HIM, all things are possible to them that believe.

No More Excuses

*The men said to Jesus, "Don't you hear what those
children are saying?"
"Yes, I do!" Jesus answered. "Don't you know that the
Scriptures say, 'Children and infants will sing
praises'?"
Matthew 21:16 (CEV)*

One of my earliest childhood memories is of attending
church with my parents, two older brothers and older sister,
who was the pianist. I remember joining the choir as a teen
to win the attention and affection of a beautiful young lady,
only to have my sister, upon hearing someone singing off-
key, pick me out of the group and ask me to leave. She knew
my real intentions.

It was the men of my church and community who stepped
in and became my male role models when my father died
when I was only fourteen. My mother, who was a devout
Christian, managed to send both my brother, who was
nicknamed "Bundy," and I to college. Her efforts were
assisted by those church members who slipped us pocket
change during our visits home. Despite having to interrupt
our college careers due to World War II, my brother and I
both graduated from Tennessee State in 1950.

Years later I would marry, become a father, find a church
home in my new Midwestern city and become a Sunday
School teacher of nine-12-year-old boys. Sunday School and
Church were a regular fixture in the lives of my family until
I changed jobs and my schedule required that I work on
Sundays. It was then that I fell out of my routine. I resigned
from my teaching position until further notice. Since my

wife who didn't drive relied on me for transportation, my family quickly became comfortable spending Sunday mornings at home. When my work schedule changed again, I joined them in their comfort zone.

A few years later, my eight-year-old daughter who had been attending Sunday School with her neighborhood friends, asked me to take her to church. I told her I would one day soon. Weeks, months, and even years passed and I had not delivered on my promise to my daughter.

It was during this time that my brother Bundy, who was the Minister of Music at a church in our hometown, was called to preach. During my brother's studies and ministerial preparation he would end our weekly phone calls with one question—Have you gone back to church yet? Soon, I will go back soon I told him. I had this request coming from two of the people closest to me, yet I didn't respond.

In 1980, shortly after Bundy received his ordination, we learned that he had cancer. The prognosis wasn't good and his time left on this earth was short. My oldest brother and I journeyed to Tennessee to visit Bundy for what would be the last time. Again, Bundy asked me when I would go back to church. Soon I told him, I'll go back soon. Bundy died on December 22, 1980, and I had yet to attend church.

Although it was my brother's dying wish for me to return to church, I didn't go back immediately. I had a ton of excuses. When my daughter asked if we could go to church one Sunday I told her I'm getting dental work and we'll go back when I get my teeth fixed. At age 11 she didn't understand what that had to do with anything. "You go to work every day," she told me. My reason, rather excuse, was that I get my teeth pulled every Friday and I need Sunday to rest and prepare for work.

By the beginning of Spring, the dental work was complete and I had become accustomed to and comfortable with my new dentures. "Can we go this Sunday?" my 11-year-old daughter asked. "This Sunday is Easter."

"Now we haven't been to church all year. It wouldn't be right to just go on Easter," I told her. She tried to make sense of this, but I knew it was senseless.

So once again I spent Easter Sunday in the comfort zone of my bedroom.

Later that week, when I was on the way home from work I got the biggest warning of my life.

At that time, I worked in the Northern Chicago Suburbs and carpooled with my son and his friend. That day I was in the car alone as both my son and his friend had the day off. On the Kennedy Expressway, in the midst of rush hour traffic a vehicle two cars in front of me came to an abrupt stop. The car in front of it stopped and I swerved slightly to avoid hitting the car in front of me. Another vehicle came behind me and pushed me further in the right lane. A car being driven by a 26-year-old newlywed hit me, and a semi-truck plowed into his vehicle.

My car was a total loss. The entire passenger side was damaged, and fortunately no one was in the passenger seat. I was blessed to be able to walk away from the accident. The newlywed wasn't as fortunate. He had to be cut out of the vehicle and sustained permanent damage. The accident made both the evening news and morning paper, and delayed traffic for over an hour.

When I finally made it home, I recounted the story to my family. My son was happy no one had been in the car with me and that I wasn't injured. My wife was happy that I was alive. My daughter's response? "Daddy, I think we need to go to church Sunday."

My three-year promise to my daughter was finally fulfilled. We started that Sunday morning in Sunday School, where I happily assumed the responsibility of teaching the nine-12-year-old boys. My daughter quickly became involved with the Young People's Department and other youth activities.

I learned to listen to my loved ones no matter how young they are, and to stop making excuses.

 # *God Doesn't Deal in Statistics*

But Jesus looked at them and said to them, "With men this is impossible, but with God all things are possible."
Matthew 19:26 (NKJV)

By all statistics I should have been a single parent on welfare, food stamps and should be offering all the excuses available for not being a productive citizen. But as God would have it, I was surrounded with positive role models in my family and extended family.

My mother was a beautiful young woman. She had grown up in a parsonage, with a wonderful loving father, an African Methodist Episcopal pastor. Her mother was a very loving Christian woman who bore ten children, five girls and five boys. One boy died at birth.

Would you believe that after bearing ten children, my grandmother was a very modest woman? She really was when it came to talking candidly to her girls about "womanhood" as they called it. She only knew to tell her girls that they should keep their skirts down and don't let boys touch them. She never explained the process of how girls grow into womanhood and how one becomes pregnant.

My mother completed ninth grade, which was as far as she could go at her school. She was such a good student that Papa and Mama (as I called my grandparents) wanted her to get the best education possible. They sent her to an African Methodist Episcopal school where she could finish her high school education. She was thrilled to have the opportunity to go away to school and was looking forward to preparing herself to become a Home Economics teacher.

While Mom was a very beautiful young woman, she was not knowledgable about sex. Upon her arrival at this school, being a Pastor's Kid, she was immediately given special attention and privileges. She worked for several faculty members cooking, doing housework, caring for their children, office work or whatever she could do to help pay for her education. She was trustworthy, so the matron allowed her to come and go whenever these faculty members requested her services.

One evening she was requested to do some office work for one of the professors. She went into the administration building to do just that, only to find that was not the purpose. As a result I was conceived. This was a difficult time for my mother as girls having children out of wedlock were scorned. For a pastor's daughter it was unforgivable. However, my grandparents stepped up to the plate and surrounded my mother with love as did her siblings.

Because of that love, my mother was able to have a calm nine month pregnancy. She said during that time she prayed for me and asked the Lord for a healthy, musically gifted baby. She had wanted to play music, but every time she got a good music teacher, they were moved to another church and town where there was not a music teacher. The Lord answered her prayers.

My biological father never tried to see me until I was seven years old. I later learned that my mother's brothers had threatened him and he knew it was not an empty threat. I didn't see him again until I was grown, married and living in Los Angeles, California. I saw his name among the delegates to the General Conference in 1960. I saw him but I didn't approach him. I am sure he saw me, as I was one of the musicians.

I thank God that my mother didn't try to abort me or give me up for adoption. I thank God that my grandparents, aunts, uncles and cousins nurtured me. Papa died when I was three years old. I remember him sitting on the side of the bed eating a bowl of soup and I watched him as he slumped over. I ran to get Mama, they took him away and I was very sad.

We lived in the parsonage, which of course was next door to the church. All our relatives came from up North. My mother's sisters and brothers had left the South and were very prosperous. People came from far and near to attend the funeral. It was a sad, but happy time. My aunts brought me pretty dresses, shoes and ribbon for my "Kitty Higgins" bow. They knew I would miss Papa because everywhere he went he would take me. It was like me and my shadow. So they surrounded me with special love.

One of my aunts was very emotional. When they brought Papa to the church to lie in state and it was time for the family to view the body she was really, really crying as she did during the funeral. The Sunday after the funeral when we were getting ready to go to worship service I said to my aunt, "There is no need for you to go to church whooping and hollering because Papa is not there, he is down the hill." God helped me to understand that Papa would not be with me any longer. How I missed him.

Immediately after Papa's death, the Church Trustees threw us out of the parsonage. They gave us exactly two weeks to find a house. As God would have it, there was one God-fearing brother on the Trustee Board who knew this was going to happen and told us of a house not too far from him that we could rent. We moved immediately. My mother was working as a receptionist for a Negro dentist making $5.50 per month. Her brother was in the CC Camp receiving a monthly stipend, and Mama was receiving fifteen dollars per quarter from the African Methodist Episcopal Church, so we were able to survive.

A few months later, while my mother was walking home one evening she met a gentleman along the way. They talked as they walked along and found that they lived not far from each other. After she talked to Mama about him, Mama told her to invite him to the house so she could see him. Mama was a strong Christian woman and knew she would be able to tell what kind of character this potential beau had. Sunday was always the time for the big family dinner, so Mama told my mother to invite him after church. Well there was one slight problem. He was Baptist. Mama loved everybody, but she didn't think anyone was going to heaven unless they were African Methodist Episcopal. Anyhow, the good brother was brave enough to come to Sunday dinner to face Mama and my two uncles who were still home. I was four at this time and able to discern a few things for myself.   We found him to be a very nice Christian man, despite being Baptist.

He was indeed a very nice person and I liked him very much. I asked my mother after they had been dating a few years, "When are you going to tie the knot?"   She told me they were thinking about it and asked me if I would like for him to be my father. I did, but you know it had to come by Mama first.

Mama said, "He seems to be a nice person, but you have to let him know that you are not going to be Baptist. He can come and join us, but you and this baby were brought up in the African Methodist Episcopal Church and that's the way it's going to be."

They married when I was six years old and we stayed with our church and he with his. However my mother would visit his church (but never with me) and he visited our church. He treated me as his very own, in fact, he spoiled me more than my mother. They never had children together because after I was born, my mother was unable to have children.

Because of my mother and my new father, I felt whole again after Papa's death. My new dad saw to it that I had everything I needed or wanted. He gave me love and encouraged me to soar. I wanted to take piano lessons and he worked extra jobs so I could get a piano. My mother continued to work, but at home, using her gift of sewing for the community.

My music was a gift from God. I could hear music and pick up the melodies by ear. My music teacher encouraged me and gave me extra time for my lessons. I was learning so fast, that by the time I was nine years old I was playing for the Sunday School. A few months later, I was playing for the Sunday morning worship.

The musician for Sunday morning worship, who played for two churches, was late as usual. On this particular Sunday, she was later than usual. It was 11:30 a.m. before she arrived. The pastor asked me if I thought I could play until she got there and I did. I knew the entire order of worship, all the hymns, and I played special music. When the pianist finally arrived he told her after the service that she didn't need to come anymore. I could do the job. I started out receiving five dollars per month and after several years they raised my salary to fifteen dollars per month. I played for the choir from elementary school, through college and for five years during my career.

My new dad was super. He was always looking out for us. His friend who worked with him at the lumber mill told him that the Cotton Belt Railroad was looking for mechanics to work on the diesel train engines. There was a class for training mechanics, had he planned to apply. It was a hot, dirty job so no white man wanted it. His friend went to the Round House, applied and was hired. A few weeks later Dad applied and was hired. After the training, his salary tripled and we thought we were rich. To top it off, we could ride on the train for free with a pass.

The free pass was for me, so this was a great help to Mama. We spent each summer up north visiting her children. School was out in May and by the first week in June, we were on our way to St. Louis, Missouri; Omaha, Nebraska and Indianapolis, Indiana. My favorite place was Omaha.

It was there that I enjoyed going to church. Mama was invited to be the visiting Stewardess and I was the visiting pianist. They had a great Youth Choir, however, they didn't sing any Gospel music. Gospel music at that time was not prevalent in the African Methodist Episcopal Church. Since I played music well by ear, I was able to pick up music by Roberta Martin, Rosetta Thorpe and the Ward singers, and teach it to the youth choir. The pastor was happy to have a little "spirit" in the service.

Because of my musical ability, I was thrown into many activities in the African Methodist Episcopal Church. The pastors and their wives mentored me at Sunday School conventions, conferences, district and connectional meetings. My first connectional meeting was the Christian Education Congress at DuSable High School in Chicago. I was accompanied by my pastor's wife, a native Chicagoan. It was there that I had an opportunity to provide the music for a reception for those in "Protocol."

A few months later at our Annual Conferencne we were assigned a new pastor and his wife who were young, well educated and lovers of children. They exposed us to every cultural experience available at that time. We felt special.

I have always been interested in the Women's Missionary Society. Mama took me as a babe to the meetings. In addition, Papa's mother was a Missionary to Africa. Mama read to me letters she had written while on her journey at a time when the only travel to West Africa was by boat. She described her hardships there, but always ended by saying the Lord was truly blessing the work. She would spend two years at a time. On her return the second time, she was stricken with a fever and died in Philadelpia. My children and I have in our possesion the last letter that she wrote.

Like most pastor's wives, I said I would never get married to a preacher. But God saw differently. Who else could I marry and enjoy the fellowship of the church of my birth? I thank God that I was "equally yoked." Because of this relationship, I have been able to share with several congregations. It is my hope that I have inspired someone to become all they could be, just as the pastors wives of my youth have inspired me.

How I got over? Love of family, mentoring by pastors and their wives during my youth, marrying the person that God ordained for my life and making and keeping lifelong friends.

No! I was not meant to be a statistic for some sociologist to hold up and predict a legacy of welfare. No! It was not meant that I should have legions of excuses as to why I didn't become. I was placed here in Divine Order. Thank you again Mother for not aborting me, not giving me up for adoption, but accepting the responsibility of being a good mother, pushing me to become the best I could be. I am truly thankful to you Mother for having the good sense to marry the love of your life, the only Dad I ever knew who was truly sent from God to form our family.

Thank you Papa and Mama for being there for my mother when she needed you most. Thank you Papa for baptizing me as a Babe and showing me by precept and example to love the Lord.

I am grateful to my God, parents and all the pastors and their wives for being my extended family. What a blessing to have been nurtured in the African Methodist Episcopal Church.

God Has a Smile
for You Too
by Nona Skiby

When I smiled at them... the light of my face was
precious to them.
Job 29:24

"I know you're talking to me Lord." That is all I kept
thinking over and over and over as the preacher kept
talking about "Absalom's House" and all the mess that was
going on in there. His message was about how you can get
caught up and feel trapped and can't see your way clear no
matter how hard you try.

I was being haunted by painful memories that would not go
away and this had been increasing now for the last two
years. It was getting to the point that when my husband
touched me, I would jump and feel the fear fresh as if I were
that eleven-year-old child again. I had been praying that the
Lord would cleanse me of all this guilt and shame.

When the preacher said, if you want to come out of your
"Absalom's House," if you want God to take you, cleanse
you, and purify you, step forward and believe God for a
miracle. I felt my feet move and my heart say, "Yes, yes,
please Lord, yes."

The next thing I knew, someone was helping me off the
floor and it felt like I was floating in air. I knew my arms
were outstretched and I could hear music. It is what I felt
that was so incredible. I felt joy unspeakable, it was so
pleasant, so clean, it was warm and I was covered in it. This

joy went inside and outside of my body all at the same time and I knew I was smiling. My soul was laughing, something that it had never done before. I looked up to the heavens and I could see God smiling at me, right into the essence of my being.

There wasn't any face, there wasn't any color, but my spirit knew that this was a smile and it was God's smile for me. It was the biggest smile ever and I was lost in it. I began to smile back until I thought I would burst into tiny atoms of joy. Every fiber of my being was tingling, I felt pure, I felt cleansed, I felt whiter than snow. I will never forget this experience.

It has been three years now since that Women's Convocation in Detroit, Michigan and the memories have disappeared. Any time I feel low or have disappointments in my life, I recall God's smile and I know He is with me and all is well.

God has a smile for you too.

Spiritual Food

They were all baptized into Moses in the cloud and in the sea. They all ate the same spiritual food and drank the same spiritual drink; for they drank from the spiritual rock that accompanied them, and that rock was Christ.
1 Corinthians 10: 2-4 (NIV)

Life in our Village is full of memories of a very special grandfather who was just a plain country preacher.

There was never a time where Grandpa was not the center, the glue if you will, who held the entire family together.

I can still see him planting and tilling his garden on the vacant lot next door to the old small home in Southern Illinois. He quietly planted and tilled his garden of corn, greens, tomatoes, onions, beans, okra, and potatoes. And of course, we had chickens running around in the backyard, for a long time I wouldn't eat chicken, to see a chicken die could be somewhat traumatic to an over imaginative child. Fortunately, I overcame that trauma; can you imagine me surviving without fried chicken?

From the garden came our daily food and nothing was wasted. Food was prepared and put into the freezer for winter months. In the yard stood an old apple tree and maple tree. A typical dinner would consist of: greens, fried corn, tomatoes, green onions, fried apple pies and they ate the "poor chicken."

This was food for our physical bodies, but most of all I remember Grandpa feeding us spiritual food.   Every

Saturday evening, all of the family would gather: aunts, uncles and especially all of the grandchildren. We gathered in the small parlor for our weekly Catechism. It was set up as a competition and as we ate popcorn made from the corn in the garden, we seriously vied for the prizes which grandpa made using bark from our trees and whittling with his pocketknife.

Of course Grandpa died long ago, but he sparked a fire in us that caused us to want to know more about Jesus, because when it is all said and done, it is "Only What You Do For Christ that Will Last."

Thanks for the memories Grandpa!

 Making Our Plates Full
by Michelle D. Belle-Villa

"Behold, how good and how pleasant it is for brethren to dwell together in unity!"
Psalm 133:1 (NKJV)

Life is packed with many challenges. We must take things one day at a time. Everyday occurrences fill our lives so that we are able to enhance the lives of others. Without realizing it, we sometimes leave a lasting impression on others. I know that on many occasions, I am so occupied with doing for others that I forget about myself. I didn't realize just how full my plate had become.

Currently, I am described as a geographical single parent with two children. My husband is in the military and deployed in another location. It is very demanding because all of the responsibilities of running our household fall upon me. I know that other individuals handle this exact situation. Needless to say, my plate is very full (as I'm sure yours is, too) and unfortunately, I was allowing my plate to devour me instead of the other way around. I became edgy and was sometimes unbearable. I became so stressed out that I wondered if I was on the verge of a nervous breakdown. God is good and He didn't allow this to happen. Instead, He armed me with the tools to get my act together and turn it around for the best.

Oftentimes we give so much of ourselves until we don't realize just how full our plates are. Here are a few things to remember that can assist with properly filling your plate. I hope that this helps others as it has helped me. I told myself that I would be receiving necessary nourishment, so:

1. Be thank_ful_.
2. Know that you are wonder_ful_.
3. Be faith_ful_
4. Be joy_ful_.
5. Be resource_ful_
6. Know that your life is event_ful_
7. You are beauti_ful_
8. Be respect_ful_.
9. Be prayer_ful_.
10. Be grate_ful_

How we fill our plates is very important. It helps us to focus on God. With this in our heart and mind, we can focus on others and ourselves. We must honor God and honor ourselves. This is what enriches our lives and makes our blessings plenti_ful_. How do you fill your plate? I am certain that you can think of other adjectives to add to this list.

God loves us and makes our lives complete! For this I am thank<u>ful</u>. I am thank<u>ful</u> because I know that where there is love, there is also hope. God knows exactly what we need and when we need it. Now isn't that enough food for thought to assist in filling your plate? Remain faith<u>ful</u> to God and be prayer<u>ful</u>. Our Merci<u>ful</u> Father blesses us with bounti<u>ful</u> blessings on a regular basis. We are all His beauti<u>ful</u> children! God made it all for the good! The depth of his gracious love is awesome and wonder<u>ful</u>! His grace and mercy assists us in making our lives <u>ful</u>filling!

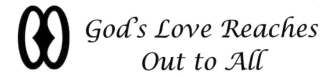 *God's Love Reaches Out to All*

***All the ways of the Lord are loving and faithful
for those who keep the demands of his covenant.
Psalm 25:10 (NIV)***

Throughout the centuries God has given people special gifts of grace, moments when God's unconditional love comes to us where we are and touches us so that we know what God is like. God enters our guilt-ridden condition, stepping not just into our "sun room" but also in the deepest cellar of our lives. God is with us just as we are, in our heights and depths, in our hours of strength and weakness—even in our times of temptation and failure. That conviction enables us to face tomorrow.

Whenever I listen to Bach, climb a hill or walk along the beach, I catch a glimpse of God. Whenever I take a child's hand, watch a sunset, gaze at the stars, or talk with a friend, I know something of the unknowable; and I realize that God's glory and love permeate every moment of our lives. In those special moments I know what God is like! And I find myself singing with the psalmist:

Praise the LORD!

O give thanks to the Lord, for he is Good
For His steadfast love endures forever.

I recall very well in my profession as a teacher, I had a student with a so-called low IQ (Intelligence Quotient). My principal demanded that I prepare the necessary papers to transfer the child to a school servicing the handicapped. In my heart I really believed that I could teach the child. For days, weeks and months I kept quiet about the child. At the end of the year he could read, write and perform math concepts. He had learned functional language and language connected with survival skills. It was my goal and practice to expose my students to the neighborhood cultural centers and activities. This young male child related to all experiences in a positive manner. He completed elementary school and continued his education at a vocational high school. I followed his progress long after he left my class. The last report I got indicated he was gainfully employed and had faithfully served one company for many years. Even though he had been considered a handicapped individual while in elementary school, he had experienced success at work when other students who were considered "normal" had failed and had to be released.

God truly reaches out to every individual, regardless of the condition. When He reaches, He only wants us to accept!

He is able to bring forth a forest in the desert. He encourages us to live faithful and be the agents for blessing others.

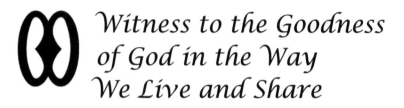

Witness to the Goodness of God in the Way We Live and Share

... Give thanks to the Lord , call on his name;
make known among the nations what he has done,
and proclaim that his name is exalted
Isaiah 12:4 (NIV)

Having faith in God signifies a connection to God's grace and living a life that reflects God's goodness.

Paul lists the following qualities of a life lived in God's goodness: true, honorable, just, pure, pleasing, commendable, excellent and praiseworthy. Then he encourages us to show these characteristics in our daily living. Jesus labeled his followers as light and salt. We are to make an impact in this world.

A story embedded in my heart is one about a schoolteacher who visited the home of one of her troublesome students. She noticed that the house was dirty and messy. The next time she visited, she brought the most beautiful plant in the world and placed it in the center of the dining table. At first, the people in the house did not realize the beauty of the plant. However, as time passed, people began to see the beauty radiated by the plant and felt a deep sense of shame about the way they kept the house. So they began to clean up and made the house fit for the beauty of the plant.

By living a life that reflects the goodness of God, we affect other people's lives. We get closer to God's kingdom when we become the agents of God's unfailing grace and mercy.

In education we have a quote: "Tell me I forget, Show me I remember, Involve me I understand." Do we really live what we say? Living out our beliefs has a deeper meaning. I once worked as a social worker. During that time I made many home visits. Most homes, especially where children live, were unkempt, and could be described as filthy dirty. I decided that I wanted to go beyond the call of duty to help the families with children. Even though my schedule was very tight because I worked days and attended evening classes, I put forth the effort to make a difference. I left home five days a week at 7:30 a.m. and returned at 10:30 p.m. I encouraged parents to do a 90-minute session to talk about health, food, and nutrition and shared community resource directories. In the process, I expressed to these parents how I had come up as a poor girl following the depression in the 1940s. My parents had love for us and very little food and clothing. But, I recalled how my mother made soap with which to clean. Our home was kept very clean. Our clothing was always clean. We had pride. Many days we had cornbread and milk for supper. However when we went to bed, we slept on clean sheets made of sackcloth.

From our discussions, my home visits reflected great change. I could sense the self-pride and self-worth making a positive difference. The children began earning better grades at school. How I got over gave me an opportunity to share with others and in so doing, helped them in their crisis of life.

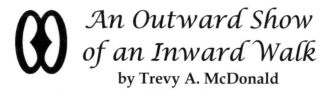

An Outward Show
of an Inward Walk
by Trevy A. McDonald

In the same way, let your light shine before men, that
they may see your good deeds and praise your Father
in heaven.
Matthew 5:16 (NIV)

It had been my long time career goal, yet I found myself
questioning if I had made the right decision. I had spent
five years preparing to become a college professor, yet when
I accepted my first tenure-track position, I wondered if I had
made the right decision. I had started graduate school
immediately following college, but I hadn't spent a great
deal of time working professionally in my field. "Am I
doing the right thing?" I asked myself as I prepared my
syllabi for the four classes to which I was assigned to teach.
I couldn't turn back. I had made a commitment to my new
job, a contractual obligation I had to meet for at least one
year.

I remember the first students I encountered upon entering
the first class I taught. It was Audio Production. I was the
new professor who had been hired over the summer that no
one knew about. With my petite frame and youthful
appearance, I was known among the media studies majors
as the professor who looked like a student.

As I prepared my lectures for class and graded assignments
critically, I began to question my choice. Here I was, under
30 and beginning my career as an educator, but wondering
if I should be working in the industry professionally to
enhance my knowledge base.

As I lectured in my classes, I was reminded of the E.F. Hutton commercials (when E.F. Hutton talks, people listen) of the mid-1970s. Students were quiet most of the time. Sometimes they copiously took notes, at other times they stared off into space. Though I tried to make the courses interactive and strongly encouraged classroom discussion, I was left wondering if I was reaching my students. I certainly needed to know well in advance of the midterm exam.

I continued to pray, and began to read the book of Proverbs, one chapter each morning. I had read Proverbs six years earlier when I first started graduate school, so surely it would give me wisdom and insight for my current experience.

One day before class a male student who was about my age asked if he could have a minute with me after class. Bobby, a conscientious student who was passionate about his discipline, had served time in the military before attending college. After the mid-term study guides were distributed, and the students cleared the room. Bobby approached me while I finished erasing the chalkboard.

"Doc, I have a personal question to ask you. Do you mind?"

This sort of caught me off guard. Surely, I thought Bobby's question had to deal with some aspect of radio station operations or audio production, or perhaps career guidance.

I braced myself, and hesitantly said, "Sure," having absolutely no idea where Bobby was headed.

"Are you a Christian?"

Automatically I responded with a resounding, "Yes." I
paused to pick up my books from the desk. "Why do you
ask?"

"I thought you were by the way you carry yourself in the
class. You're very different from some of the other
professors. You're very patient and have a sense of peace
about you."

While Bobby did not say I was an excellent teacher or
comment on the material he was learning from me, his
question was an affirmation for me. From that day forward,
my attitude about my job was different. Each moment I
interacted with my students, I was not focused only on
teaching them the tools they needed to obtain a job in the
field, but on letting my inward walk show on the outside.

Courage

The Goodness of God
by Mary Laws

But let all who take refuge in you be glad; let them ever sing for joy. Spread your protection over them, that those who love your name may rejoice in you
Psalm 5:11 (NIV)

One day a co-worker who sings in our church choir and I were to attend a funeral during our lunch hour. On our way, we were driving down a one-way street to the funeral home when all of a sudden a blue car appeared and sideswiped us. My co-worker swerved and we went over the curb and then under a guide wire. The car landed in a parking lot between two parked cars. Amazingly we did not hit either car.

We sat silently for a few minutes to gather ourselves, and then we thanked the Lord for His protection.

People came from everywhere to look at what they called a miracle. They brought yardsticks to measure the distance between the guide wire and the parked cars.

We were blessed to be alive and through the goodness of God there was no damage to the car. We knew that God had something more He wanted us to do and we were committed to be about our Father's work.

God is good, all the time, God is good.

I Ain't Mad at God
by Lorenzo C. Robertson

---

*And we know that all things work together for good to
them that love God, to them who are the called
according to his purpose.*
Romans 8:28 (KJV)

I was created in the image of a caring, compassionate and
loving God; deemed to be a person who reflects that image,
and I strive to be the person. The person He created me to
be on His earth. About five years ago I was dealt a
devastating blow that changed the way I lived my life. I
was diagnosed with AIDS. That day that literally changed
the way I viewed life, as precious as it was I often took it for
granted. Hearing the doctor say, "You've got AIDS,"
changed my life forever. Three words! No, it didn't make
me bitter it made me better. I am not mad—I'm a miracle.
I'm his child and from that day I have asked the Lord to
keep me in His arms of protection, but never once asked
why me?

Instead I asked myself why not me. Obviously, God knew
that I could handle the pressures and challenges that
ultimately would be ahead for me and my family and my
friends. With prayers and support from people that love
and care about me, I have embarked upon this journey as a
person living with AIDS. I have opted not to flip the script
and pretend that AIDS doesn't exist in my life. Instead, I
have just decided that I would not allow AIDS to dictate my
life and all that I want to do with it.

Through it all I have learned to lean on the everlasting and ever strong arms of God. He has held me when there was no one there to hold me. He has comforted me in my lowest hours when I didn't feel that living a life with AIDS was worth living. The Lord has kept me from opportunistic infections, major complications or serious illnesses. Unfortunately, I can't say the same for others who have had to travel the same road. So I know that the Lord has a song for me to sing, praise to worship and testimony that is sure to glorify His name. It is called living.

Five years and a little further on the journey, I'm living the life that I was afraid to live before. AIDS is a devastating disease and many people are afraid to even utter the word. I am *not* one of those people. I have even taken it one step further. I also work in the AIDS field. I am currently an administrator for an AIDS service organization, which serves mostly Black clients. I have learned that our people, Black and religious people, are some of the people that are most afraid of AIDS. In my professional capacity I try to desensitize Black people about a subject that is many times swept under the rug and never ever spoken about in mixed company (anyone outside the family).

I ain't mad at God for the things that He has allowed to happen in my life. I am grateful. Grateful that I am still here to praise the Lord one more time. Grateful that I can glorify His name to the highest. Grateful that I can make a difference in the lives of those who live with this disease and those who don't understand it. Grateful that He has kept me here for the purpose for which He has called me. Grateful that I know that AIDS was not a punishment because God was mad a me ... and I ain't mad at God. Amen.

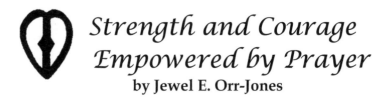

Strength and Courage Empowered by Prayer
by Jewel E. Orr-Jones

Have I not commanded you? Be strong and courageous. Do not be terrified; do not be discouraged, for the LORD your God will be with you wherever you go."
Joshua 1:9 (NIV)

I was the area Young People's Department (YPD) Director when my daughter was diagnosed with an incurable illness. She was only ten years old and I was told she would not grow or walk anymore. We took her to the Mayo Clinic after many stays at the Hospital in Racine, WI.

During her third visit to the Mayo Clinic, her heart and lungs stopped, but we were always in prayer. That night we thought she was going to die. But we weren't praying alone. Reverend and Mrs. Thomas Cooper of Wayman Church, the YPDers, and the Missionary Society prayed without ceasing.

Praise be to God she did not die that night. Wayman had an all night prayer vigil. We were in intensive care for six weeks and my daughter not only left the Mayo Clinic walking, she grew, graduated from high school on time, got married, and has two children.

She had been told she would never have children. My daughter is a miracle living today and I give thanks to God, my church, and the WMS/YPD for praying for my family and me.

Lynda's Story
by **Mary Fleming Hughes**

Fret not thyself because of evildoers, neither be thou envious against the workers of iniquity. For they shall soon be cut down like the grass and wither as the green herb.
Psalm 37:1-2 (KJV)

One of my friends, Lynda (not her real name), was a victim of domestic violence. I found out from her mother that her husband, Mark (not his real name), was emotionally and physically abusing her on a regular basis. Yes, he was tall, dark, handsome, college-educated, and a Christian. However, Mark was also a jealous control freak and demanded to know Lynda's whereabouts each minute of the day. If he called her office and she was away from her desk, he would get very suspicious and sometimes slap her when she came home. To avoid this, Lynda would try her best to let Mark know when she would be in a meeting or at lunch. He accused her of having an affair and threatened to kill her. No matter how Lynda tried to please Mark, he grew more physically abusive.

When I tried to talk with Lynda, she would deny the abuse and insisted that Mark loved her. My concern for Lynda's safety increased after one of Mark's beatings put her in the hospital with three broken ribs. She recovered and went home to Mark. Soon after, I saw them at a political affair and Lynda had a new mink coat.

I said, "Nice coat."

She replied, "A gift from Mark."

Six months later, Lynda gained enough courage to leave Mark. She and her son from a previous marriage moved in with her mother. Mark called and threatened her life despite the fact that she had taken out a peace bond on him. One day as she was on her way to work, Mark grabbed her from behind and threw her into his car. He drove around with Lynda for hours trying to convince her that he would get help for his temper and how much he loved her. When she refused to take him back, he stabbed her repeatedly.

Mark drove to his sister's home with Lynda barely alive. His sister then drove Lynda to the hospital where she was pronounced dead. She had lost too much blood. If he had only taken her to the hospital earlier she would have lived. Mark went into hiding for two weeks until he had his legal defense in place. In less than two months, he was found not guilty of murder.

How could I live with this injustice? I remembered Psalm 37 and the verse "Fret not thyself because of evildoers..."

Approximately 1.5 million women are assaulted by their current or former partner in this country. About 2,000 are killed. If you know someone who is a victim of domestic violence, please let them know they are not alone and there is help. Domestic violence is a crime. The National Domestic Violence Hotline is 1-800-SAFE. Do it for Lynda.

More Than
Just The Blues
by C.L. Poindexter

Your sun shall no longer go down, nor shall your moon
withdraw itself;
For the Lord will be your everlasting light, and the
days of your mourning shall be ended."
Isaiah 60:20 (NKJV)

I am an African American woman! Proud, beautiful, educated, and God-fearing. I come from a close-knit family. I have lots of close friends. I date. I am surrounded in love. Most people who know me, know all of this. What most people don't know, however, is that in the summer of 1998 I was diagnosed with clinical depression.

For the most part I kept everything hidden. I continued to play the role of the outgoing, funny, active woman that everyone expected me to be. Even when depression among black women was discussed within my sorority I said nothing. Deciding to put my story in print form is even harder for me.

Due to the negativity associated with mental health problems in the black community it had taken me almost a year to finally seek professional help. In the meantime I thought I could help myself. Often the feelings of overwhelming sadness would come and go. I would have my good days and my bad days. I thought I would just "snap out of it" but it never happened. I read the Bible, prayed, read motivational books, went to church, and even blamed it on PMS. Eventually my emotional and even my physical health were so weak that I finally admitted that it was more than "just the blues."

There are many signs that could be attributed to depression, such as:

> overwhelming feelings of sadness or emptiness
> irritability
> weight loss or weight gain
> insomnia or excessive sleepiness
> lack of energy
> difficulty concentrating
> suicidal thoughts
> lack of interest in daily activities

Depression can affect individuals from all walks of life, however African Americans, particularly African American women, are the least likely to seek help. If any of the above symptoms arise and last for a period of two weeks or longer, there is a good chance that depression may exist. If you or anyone that you know is suffering from any of the above symptoms I urge you to seek help. If not treated, depression can destroy your quality of life, affect your physical health, even result in suicide. It is speculated that the majority of individuals who commit suicide were suffering from depression. In June of 1995 one of my all time favorite singers, Phyllis Hyman, committed suicide just hours before she was scheduled to perform at the Apollo Theatre in New York. She had been severely depressed for quite some time.

The first step in my path to healing was to admit that I needed professional help. That was one of the hardest things

I have ever had to do. I really had to pray about it and ask God to direct my path. That is when I realized that God gives us tools in which to deal with life's battles. In my case God sent me a wonderful therapist. God gave me the strength to make the phone call that I needed to make in order to seek help.

When my therapist uttered the words, "You are suffering from clinical depression," all I could do was stare at her. Although I was the one who made the appointment to see her, I still had a little bit of denial left in me. I couldn't figure out how I had arrived at this point in my life. I was never abused or molested; I had never used drugs. I couldn't pin point why I was so unhappy. In therapy I learned a great deal about myself, which was funny since I previously thought I knew everything there was to know about me. I learned that I should be more open with my feelings. I learned that I do not have to take on the role of superwoman. I learned that I have to make time for myself and put myself first. I learned how to better deal with stress. I learned that it's okay to feel sad, it's okay to cry. Most importantly I learned that seeking professional help was not a sign of weakness. Suffering from depression is not a sign of weakness. Depression is a disease, and like most diseases, it needs effective treatment. With the proper treatment depression can be cured.

Although I sought professional help, my depression is something that I continue to deal with. I continue to utilize professional help, when needed. I still have my good days and my bad days. I now have more good days than bad, and now I am better equipped to handle the bad days.

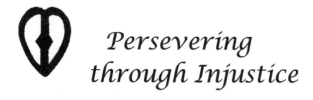

Persevering through Injustice

O magnify the Lord with me and let us exalt His name together
Psalm 34:3 (KJV)

The focal point of my narrative is about obtaining a Masters degree in Educational Administration from an all white male Catholic institution. This incident took place during the height of the Civil Rights Movement for equality and justice in the Midwest.

I was a third grade teacher in the local Public school system, an active participant in the Civil Rights Movement and a member of the NAACP during my late husband's tenure as its president. I served as a member of the Urban League's Board (Women's Division).

The Indiana State Board of Education required all teachers to obtain a Master's degree after teaching five years in the state. This posed a problem for me as there were no higher educational institutions nearby. This meant I would have to relocate to another area of the state or change my profession.

About the same time, the President of the University announced to the NAACP that it was having open enrollment in its graduate program for all nuns, Protestants and minorities. I, along with some nuns, other blacks and Hispanics enrolled in evening, summer and Saturday classes because we were employed during the day. That is when racism and injustice reared their ugly heads. Most of us had been active participants in several protest marches in the city.

I faced many challenges, endured subtle racial implications, and became aggressive in getting the good grades comparable to the quality of my work. Some problems became so glaring that several classmates banded together for prayer before confronting teachers about several other issues. Eventually, several professors were either terminated or demoted in rank.

At last, graduation day had arrived; I was the second female of color to graduate with an M.A. in Educational Administration. The President gave special commendations to the women who endured to the end. Several other civic and social groups joined in celebratory activities.

Kept in Peace
by Marjorie L. Kimbrough

Thou wilt keep him in perfect peace, whose mind is stayed on thee; because he trusteth in thee.
Isaiah 26:3 (KJV)

I found myself sitting in the pre-operation room in the summer of 1998. I was scheduled for breast cancer surgery, and I was completely at peace. My husband, a United Methodist minister, had been with me earlier to pray with and anoint me. I knew Jesus was with me and would heal me as He said. His promises are true, and my faith is strong.

There was another patient awaiting the same surgery. She was tossing and turning and constantly calling to the nurses for blankets and other items of comfort. While one of the nurses was trying to comfort her, she looked over at me and said, "I wish I could be at peace like that lady. She is so calm." The nurse responded, "Yes, she is at peace, and I want you to be that way."

The patient explained all the many complications surrounding her case and the many stresses under which she had been because of her husband's cancer-ridden body. She just knew she would not experience a complete recovery. She was not expecting her miracle of peace, and she did not experience it. Somehow it is always true that we must expect miracles to receive them.

I do not know how her surgery turned out, but I did pray that she would know the promises of Jesus and realize peace within her spirit. As I thought about that woman I kept praising God and thanking Him for the healing that I knew was being evidenced in my own body and for the faith my husband and I stand on. We know about and claim His miraculous healing power. We always expect a miracle!

It is wonderful to be kept in peace, and we can be if we keep our minds stayed on God. Terrorists cannot disturb or upset us if we know who is keeping us. Let there be peace on earth, and let it begin with each of us.

The Lord Brushed My Teeth
by Evelyn E. Farris

Nay, in all these things we are more than conquerors through Him who loves us.
Romans 8:37 (KJV)

My widowed mother lived in my home and my three sisters and I shared the responsibilities for her care. I was employed as a silk finisher. I followed my usual daily routine on February 19, 1977, first brushing my teeth and then showering before heading off to work as my sister came to give Mama her insulin injection. The toothpaste dripped off the brush onto my yellow gown. I tried to wipe it off, only to discover a pink spot on my gown near the nipple of my left breast. My breast had a pinkish discharge.

All my morning plans changed. With my mother's insistence, my sister and I hurried to the hospital emergency room. The medical personnel were confused as to what to do. My doctor was not in, he was teaching at the Medical School that morning. When he was contacted he told me to meet him at his office in Zion, Illinois in just over an hour. When I got there, he probed and prodded but could not detect anything seemingly abnormal. He could not feel any lumps anywhere. He sent me back to the hospital to determine if a biopsy should be performed. Several mammograms were done. Things were now moving quickly. The biopsy revealed fatty tissue in the lower portion of my left breast had become cancerous!

The doctor told me flat out, "Your breast will have to be removed immediately!" A total mastectomy. But today that would not be necessary with the strides medical science has made. The next day as I was rolled into the operating room, the nurse tried to comfort me by telling me not to be afraid. My reply to her came from my conviction that as I had lived I was now speaking. I said, "I am not frightened. I am not going in there alone because Jesus is going with me." The doctor was already amazed that I had not become morose nor terrified and commented that I was an excellent candidate and he wished all of his patients had my attitude. I knew I felt no fear. I was confident that this was in line with my faith as a believer. I had no time to be afraid. I attempted to brush my teeth and noticed the discharge on Wednesday, had the biopsy on Thursday and surgery was being performed on Friday.

I awakened after being in recovery long enough to observe my three sisters at my bedside and my mother wearing a green dress seated next to the bed. I reached for my mother's hand and with my other hand I felt for the breast that had been removed. I didn't say anything. I went back to sleep. My mother, my three sisters and my employer were there constantly giving me support and surrounding me with their love. It was no surprise that the healing was rapid and I was soon ready to go home. I asked the doctor when would I begin my chemotherapy treatments. He replied there would be no treatments. I was cancer free. Two weeks later I was in attendance at the North Area Conference Branch meeting, of which I was the Area Chairperson.

I consistently have my annual mammograms and do regular examinations. The same God who "brushed my teeth and dripped the toothpaste" that Wednesday morning has faithfully kept me cancer free. I am more than a breast cancer survivor, I am a conqueror through Him who loves me. I praise my healer, my conquering King!

The Night the Angels Sang
by Julia A. Hagwood

... "Fear not, for I have redeemed you;
I have summoned you by name; you are mine.
When you pass through the waters,
I will be with you;
and when you pass through the rivers,
they will not sweep over you...
Isaiah 43:1-2 (KJV)

I had cried myself to sleep. In the wee hours of the morning I awakened. I had been dreaming, but more than that I was hearing music—a hymn. I hummed the tune to myself and thought about the words. I realized the song was "How Firm a Foundation." Such sleep as I had been able to get had come through medication. My heart was broken. Everyone who knew us was aware of the deep love my husband and I shared in our marriage. My most beloved husband was at that moment struggling for life in a cardiac care unit having suffered a massive heart attack. Even after being awake, I could still hear what sounded like angels singing.

I checked my bedside radio to see if the Christian radio station had been left on. It was off. The television was also off. I was home alone. The music persisted. It sounded like a full choir. I reached for my Bible saying aloud to myself,

"That's Scripture, I want to find it." I found 2 Timothy 2:19 and Isaiah 43:1-2. For days and weeks and months I received the same message *daily* as we petitioned the Lord for my husband's recovery: "Fear Not, I am With You."

Among the scores of cards and notes of comfort we received repeatedly, Isaiah 43:1-2 was printed on them affirming the song the angels sang.

Of all the attributes of God it is His faithfulness that continually astounds me. His promise to strengthen, help and cause me to stand upheld by his righteous omnipotent hand has been real. My husband lingered and slowly wasted away until his death 16 months to the day he was stricken. At this writing it has been over 10 years. The night the angels sang "at home and abroad, on the land, on the sea, as thy days may demand, shall thy strength ever be. Then the rivers of woe shall not thee overflow. For I will be with the thy troubles to bless, And sanctify to thy deepest distress." I have a fondness for hymns and desire to sing every verse in worship services. Each verse of this hymn is special music to my soul as I remember the night the angels sang to me.

 *Alpha and Omega*
by Sharon J. Brumfield

I am Alpha and Omega, the beginning and the ending, saith the Lord, which is, and which was, and which is to come, the Almighty.
Revelation 1:8 (KJV)

"Young, Beautiful, Educated Black Woman" was brushed in gold across the black cotton shirt, but Rebekah put it down to reach for a brighter souvenir. "I'll take this one," she told the vendor. The shirt was white with "I am Alpha and Omega" in orange and pink neon letters.

The Women's Missionary Society Quadrennial had just ended and Robert was loading the trunk in the parking area outside of the Hall. We had checked out of the hotel before noon and were prepared for the long drive back to Baton Rouge. I commented on how beautiful the weather had been since we left Michigan and calculated our dinner stop would be in Nashville. Rebekah and Stephen slept most of the trip, seat belted and covered in YPD green bath sheets with pillows to cushion their heads. They woke up frequently as the highway got bumpier, but always tuned into familiar songs. From Motown to Memphis, we eased down the road sharing prayer and music with Rebekah and Stephen.

When we crossed the Mississippi River, Stephen was singing Gatemouth Moore's song, "I Ain't Mad at You Pretty Baby." It was after midnight so not going to Beale Street was a disappointment for Rebekah. We kept on singing, driving through Tennessee and were two exits north of Grenada, Mississippi. I told Robert we needed to stop for gas and to let the kids take a nature break. The cashier bagged the gum and apple juice and soon we were on our way. The Memphis radio station had faded with the distance, but the scanner went right to the Jackson station. We drove down Interstate 55 South, just four hours away from the parsonage in Baton Rouge. There was church business for Robert to get back to, and my father had been hospitalized in New Orleans.

The Boys II Men tune was playing and I chimed in on "Don't Wait Till the Water Runs Dry." The road marker read Holmes County and I glanced at the clock. It was 4:27 a.m. when the tire exploded. The car screeched as we skidded sideways down the middle of the road. The children screamed as the car scraped against the trees. Seat belt cuts and the cool mist from the airbag awakened me, and Robert was strangely reclined with his head resting in Stephen's lap. Both Rebekah and Stephen were calling for us as they dusted glass from their pillows. Robert and I tried to assure them that everything would be all right.

"I'll get out and get some help," Rebekah said as she squeezed between her door and the bushes. I could not find the cell phone so I called for her to wait for me, not realizing my right knee ligaments had been torn.

"I'll stay with Daddy," Stephen said as he shook the glass from his towel to cushion his father's head.

I crawled up the hill to where Rebekah stood waving her arms. "Just wait until you see some headlights approaching," I told her as I sat helplessly on the soft grass. The first vehicle that stopped was a white Jeep. The young white couple was dressed in white clothing and hurried to check our condition. I could hear the gentleman asking

Robert and Stephen if they were okay. The young woman ran to the Jeep to call for help. The second vehicle to stop was an eighteen-wheeler truck. A tall man dressed in dark clothing got out and looked us over, he then hurried back only to climb into the truck and quickly drive away. "That was weird," I commented to the lady who remained with us. "What made you stop?" I asked her. She said she saw this flash of white on the side of the road and as she and her fiancé got closer they could see Alpha and Omega in huge neon letters. Then she saw Rebekah's waving arms and our car embracing a tree in the shadows.

The Mississippi state trooper had called for the "jaws of life" and an ambulance after he could not open Robert's door. He was shaking his head when he handed me Robert's jewelry, and Stephen reassured us that we would all be fine. The ambulance crossed the median quickly as Robert moaned in pain, and our kids rode in the front seat with the driver as I swallowed to loosen the neck brace.

A few hours had passed, and I called the nurse to give directions to the small hospital over the phone. A minister friend of ours followed the ambulance to the hospital where Robert and I could be treated. The emergency room was crowded, but we stayed together until our friend took our children to his home in Jackson. I was getting weaker and my knee had swollen so much. After X-rays, we were finally taken to a private room where Robert was resting a bit. I noticed tiny red bumps all around my swollen knee, and dead fire ants were attached to my pant legs.

We were driven back to Baton Rouge a week or so later, where our church family and cousins nurtured us back to health. Two weeks later I was getting dressed for my father's funeral when I realized I had sat in a bed of fire ants on the side of the road. The ant bites were only around my knee, as if they had been purposely located to bite in that area. Our merciful God in His infinite wisdom had those fire ants on I-55 just waiting for me! Their bites prevented a killer blood clot from forming.

Rebekah is now a college sophomore and Stephen a high school junior. God has blessed us and expanded our territory by sending us to minister in Detroit.

I am thankful for Rebekah's courage to go up that hill in the dark and for Stephen's faith as he comforted his father in the car with no lights. I still don't remember the actual impact of the car as it crashed into that big pine tree. But I do remember that we should all have faith in God, the Alpha and Omega, The Beginning and the End.

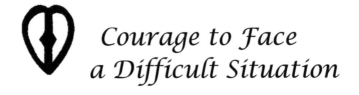

Courage to Face a Difficult Situation

For God has not given us a spirit of fear, but of power and of love and of a sound mind.
2 Timothy 1:7 (NJKV)

The toes on my right foot severely shifted to the extreme right over a period of several years. My toes began to stack on top of each other and caused me to experience extreme discomfort. I was afraid to have surgery and ignored the signs of progressive degeneration.

I prayed and asked God to give me courage and direction regarding my problem. I also asked him to eliminate the spirit of fear from my mind. Most of all, I prayed that His will would be done.

The Lord removed the spirit of fear from my mind and directed me to an excellent podiatrist. In August 2000, I solicited the prayers of the Women's Missionary Society Michigan Annual Conference Branch attendees and underwent surgery a few days later on my right foot. All of my toes were broken and straightened on my right foot. I remained in the hospital for one day without complications. When I returned home, I experienced minimal pain and the recovery process was successful. I can now wear a shoe comfortably on my right foot.

Having a Cause
by Michelle D. Belle-Villa

Happy are those who find wisdom... She is a tree of life to those who lay hold of her; those who hold fast are called happy .
Proverbs 3:13, 18 (NKJV)

We should all love the skin that we are in. Well, I have to admit, there were many times in my life that I didn't like my features at all. My peers made me an object of ridicule. This is spoken from a black woman that is not so black. I am very light complexioned with sandy brown hair and blue-gray eyes. Call me a true blue-eyed soul sister, but years ago I felt like a blue-eyed monster.

Other than my family members and a few (I stress few) children in my neighborhood, no one wanted to have anything to do with me. "Redbone, high yellow, and throw back" were the taunting names associated with me. I didn't think it would ever stop. Those words smarted worse than any bee sting and broke down my self-esteem while tearing away at my spirit as well. Sure, there were other light-skinned family members, but none of them had the blue-gray eyes! I longed for deep cocoa brown skin, black hair and dark brown eyes. This is what I considered necessary to possess beauty.

When integration of schools came along, there were additional problems. This meant redistricting and having to get to know an entirely new set of children. The white children didn't want to play with me because I wasn't white enough and the black children didn't want to play with me because they felt I was "light bright, almost white." I became an outcast and the others would only play with me during the group activities that the teachers coordinated.

The fact that my father was not present in my life did not help matters. This brought the assumption that perhaps my father was white. This is not the case and my mother explained that I looked like my great-great-grandfather. A product of the grandfather ancestry trait, these features show up once every four generations. I accepted the explanation, but my mind only allowed me to think the worst. One look in the mirror filled me with sadness. I questioned God and His reason for making me the way I am. In time the answer would be revealed to me...in God's time.

Over the years, I have grown to accept my looks and adapted to my environment. Yes, it is quite possible that I am a reminder of the history of our culture, but perhaps a symbol of our strength and how far people of color have come as well. Through prayer and God's mercy I possess the courage to persevere. It was necessary for me to learn self-acceptance. Our Omnipotent Father prepared me.

Through these trials (self-pity, poor self-esteem), God was arming me with courage, nurturing me, intensifying my faith, increasing my wisdom and guiding me to the road of self-acceptance. What a triumph! I realized my cause. We all have to realize our cause...COURAGE AND UNDER-STANDING SUPPLY ENCOURAGEMENT. We are all beautiful in the sight of the Lord, thus we should not lose sight of Him. He uses us everyday. I know there are other individuals that can relate to my words. God has given me the strength and courage to share these words... that are deeply personal to me. I say to you, "Be encouraged! Have CAUSE!" God makes it so!

 Tea for Two

I have given you authority to trample on snakes and scorpions and to overcome all the power of the enemy; nothing will harm you.
Luke 10:19 (NIV)

It happened a lifetime, or two ago, but I remember that day, just like it was yesterday. I grew up in a small, coal mining, company-owned town in West Virginia during the Depression. Our house sat on the bank of Kelly's Creek. Papa's day job was in the mines, and on Sundays he sat in the pulpit of Mount Zion Baptist Church. While we were poor, as was everyone in our town, our family was happy, healthy and we shared a close bond.

I was number nine of thirteen children, the next to youngest girl in a family of seven boys and six girls and the only child in the family with a speech impediment. Our evenings were spent around the radio listening to *Mystery Theater* and *The Shadow*, after Papa read the Bible to us. A fork was not lifted around the dinner table until Papa had finished blessing the food and each of my siblings and I recited a Bible verse. My brother Nehemiah's favorite was Acts 10:13, "Rise Peter slay and eat."

I spent my days during my early childhood helping my mother around the house while my older siblings were at school. One sunny fall afternoon in 1931 when I was four years old I helped my mother carry her canned goods into our makeshift cellar underneath our house. When Mama finished storing her Mason jars, she gave me permission to play down there with my tea set. She headed back into our house when she saw our next-door neighbor who struck up a conversation.

I carefully set my teacups and saucers on the cool floor of the cellar. When I stopped to pour my imaginary tea into a cup, I discovered I had company. Shades of tan and brown, with an hourglass pattern and a head the shape of a diamond, it sat coiled in the corner of the room. It looked at me with its light brown eyes similar to a cat. I was up close and personal with an uninvited guest, and I was scared. I left my tea and ran up into the backyard to tell my mother.

My speech impediment was stuttering and it took forever for me to get the first syllables out, but once they were out, I ran through the remainder of my sentence as if I were an Olympic sprinter. I ran over to Mama, pulled on the bottom of her dress interrupting her conversation and said, "M-m-m--m-m-m-mama, the-res a snakeunderthehouse."

"Go on back and play child," Mama told me. And being an obedient four-year-old, I did just that.

I went back into the cellar, and my visitor was still there. I felt a sense of calm and peace, and I quietly continued to play with my tea set. Although I know now that I was in a dangerous situation for some reason I felt safe. But my mind told me that I needed to try and let Mama know about the snake again.

I went back into the yard, this time more persistent. "M-m-m-m-mm-mama, theres a snake underthehouse."

"Did you hear what your child just said?" the neighbor asked. "She said there's a snake under your house. You need to go and see about that."

Mama quickly ended her conversation and took a look for herself.   Coiled in the corner was a copperhead, one of America's venomous snakes.

"Don't go back down there baby," she instructed me.

Mama saw two men walking down the road in front of our house enroute to the company store and enlisted their help. While they appeared to be afraid of the snake, they were successful in killing it.

I am certain now, as I was at four years old, that an angel was present with me under the house that day who kept me safe from harm.

Mother's Day Mayday
by Dana Burns Smith

Now unto him that is able to do exceeding abundantly above all that we ask or think, according to the power that worketh in us.
Ephesians 3:20 (KJV)

On Sunday May 9, 1999, I delivered identical twin girls – Meagan Arnell and Morgan Adele by C-section. They were seven weeks early. Meagan weighed 4 lbs. 3 ozs. and Morgan weighed 3 lbs. 9 ozs. The miracle in all this is that I have no memory of their birth or the week to follow. I was diagnosed with Lupus during my pregnancy and was being monitored closely.

The day started out as any other great Mother's Day, but as the day progressed I began having abdominal pain. I thought it was indigestion, so I started eating TUMS like candy. Little did I know the Lord was setting everything into motion. I finished packing my bag for the hospital, even though I was not due until June 28th and sent my girlfriend, Karolyn to the grocery store to pick up a few items for the house. She also brought me lunch and balloons and went on her way. I sent my older daughter,

Maya to church with my sisters Rona and Trish.   My husband, Chester was at work. I found myself home alone and the pain was getting worse.

By this time my mother called (not knowing I was in distress) and said she was on her way. I was relieved, but I couldn't wait. I called 911 and my doctor because I knew something wasn't right. When the ambulance arrived, they couldn't take me to the hospital of my choice for reasons I did not want to hear at the time. Thankfully, my mother arrived just in the time—as she always did. She drove me to the hospital. I collapsed in pain in the elevator. My doctor and the nurses were waiting for me. When I showed her where the pain was she told Chester, "It's her liver, we're going to have to take the babies," and that's all I remember until the following Saturday when I woke up in ICU.

Doctor Adam explained to me that when she cut me for the C-section my liver had ruptured. The trauma and loss of blood caused my heart to stop and my bodily functions started shutting down. I was resuscitated and placed on a ventilator to help me breathe. They tell me my husband and family were devastated. I went in awake to have my babies and the next time they saw me I was unconscious and swollen almost beyond recognition. I received numerous blood transfusions. I was told later that I held the record for the most blood and blood products given at this particular hospital. Since my blood stopped clotting, they had to do exploratory surgery and pack my insides with gauze in an effort to stop the bleeding. I was told the bleeding stopped three days later, but the doctors still couldn't understand why I wasn't waking up. My family was told that if I survived I would be a vegetable, on dialysis or in need of a liver transplant.   They said my chances for survival were slim and that the only thing I had going for me was that I was young. The doctor's didn't know I had more than that going for me.

I am a child of the King and God takes care of His children. The Lord knew I had a husband and a two-year old daughter who needed me. A mother, sisters and friends who relied on me and a great deal of saints were praying for me, including my grandmother. My husband said even the Chaplain seemed to give up hope, but he had made a deal with the Lord that he would stop running from his calling if He let me live.

The following Saturday morning, my mother and older sister walked in as they said they did most mornings, but this time when they said hello Dana, I said, "Hey!!!!!!!" That is the first new memory that I have –seeing the look on their faces. I could barely speak because of the tubes in my mouth and nose. They quickly called Chester to come. When he got there all he could do was cry and everybody else that came after him cried also. At this point I was informed that I had delivered the twins and they were in NICU at another hospital. This left me confused because I had two separate incisions—one that I knew was the C-section and the other looked like I had been cut wide open. The doctor did not explain all that I had been through until the next day. It overwhelmed me. Now when I think about it, it still amazes me how God allowed me to lay there all those days and then just decided to reach down from Heaven and wake me up so He could get the glory.

Yes, to God be the glory for all the things that He has done. He spared my life and gave me another chance to be better. In man's eye my ship was sinking, but God said otherwise. The family of God yelled "MAYDAY," and He stepped in and calmed the sea. My twins celebrated their third birthday, Maya is preparing for first grade, Chester accepted his calling to the ministry and all is well. We are all healthy and praising God for the victory. However, my mother recently passed away, so I'm waiting on the Lord to work His magic as He always does and help me through this storm as only He can.

Healing Emotional Wounds
by Pauline M. Rivers

Sharp words cut like a sword,
but words of wisdom HEAL.
Proverbs 12:18 (CEV)

"You have been wounded deeply, by things people have done to you and said to you and it has caused you to become introverted and withdraw into a shell. But, I am sending healing and peace into your life. It is time to take off the sackcloth of mourning, for I will break alive in you."

These words were spoken to me 12 years ago when I visited a small full gospel church in Chapel Hill, North Carolina. The pastor had called all of the single women up for prayer, and even though I didn't belong to that church, I responded to the altar call. I met up with destiny at that altar.

"Wounded deeply. By things people have done and said. But, I am sending healing and peace..."

I wept freely, unashamedly, and cathartically, as the pastor spoke those words to me. I knew the voice of God was speaking through him to me. And, I knew God understood. He understood my pain. He saw my wounds and the scars that covered my wounds. He saw my suitcase full of hurts, the painful memories that I carried with me always. He knew that I needed to be healed and that I wanted to be healed, but I didn't know how. So, God spoke a word to me that touched the secret places of my heart; a word so clear and revealing that I knew it came from Him. It was a word that gave me hope and set me on a course for being healed from emotional wounds.

It would be great if the story had ended there. It would be great if I could say that I grabbed my healing and walked in complete victory from that day forward. But, it didn't happen that way. There was more for me to learn on my journey to being healed from emotional wounds. I got a quick fix that day, 12 years ago. I received an emotional release and left the church rejoicing. But, I didn't have complete understanding and I didn't know how to keep my healing. So, when things that people said or did to me wounded me again, deeply, I withdrew into my familiar shell. I erected a wall to keep me safe from people who might hurt me again. And every time I would replay a memory about someone who had hurt me, betrayed me, offended me, or disappointed me, I would fortify my wall, build it higher, thicker, and wider.

An interesting relationship developed between my walls and my memories. The more I thought about who did what to me and when, the higher my walls got. My walls and my memories worked together to keep me safe from fresh wounds, *or so I thought*. I couldn't let go of my memories. I couldn't forget. I was afraid to forget, because if I forgot, somebody might hurt me again.

For years I continued with this pattern of replaying the memories and fortifying the wall, replaying the memories and fortifying the wall. It was working out. I had a good life, good husband, wonderful children, nice house at the country club, growing consulting business, and a small circle of trusted friends. But, funny thing is, it only takes one phone call to change your world.

My phone call came one Friday evening when I found out that someone was coming back into my life that I had hoped I would never have to deal with again in this lifetime. The wounds from that relationship were so painful that I often thought that if I never see this person again until we both get to heaven, that will be just fine with me. I believe within my heart and with my every fiber that I had forgiven this person, but I didn't want her in my life again. I wasn't bitter, but I was still hurting and I felt that the best way to protect myself was to just not see this person again, until we got to heaven.

But, she was coming back into my life and we weren't in heaven. I was going to have to deal with her, and my issues surrounding her, here on earth. All of the memories of our painful past came flooding over me at once. It was too much. I felt overwhelmed and completely helpless. There was nothing I could do to stop this from happening and I was scared.

And so, I did what I know to do when I am afraid, and when a problem is too big for me. (*When I am afraid, I will trust in you. In God, whose word I praise, in God I trust; I will not be afraid. What can mortal man do to me? Psalm 56:34, NIV*). I woke up early one Sunday morning, went into my secret place, and had a talk with God, my Abba Father, my

Daddy. I told him that I was scared. I told Him that I wanted to be healed, but I didn't know how. I wanted the deep wounds underneath and the scars on the outside to be healed. I told him that I wanted more than a quick fix and an emotional release. I wanted concrete, tangible steps that I could take so that I could be healed completely from the inside out.

I prayed. God answered. Healing flowed. I was so hungry for direction and for healing that I wrote down every thing that God, through the Holy Spirit, spoke to me that Sunday morning. I read over those *"steps to healing emotional wounds"* three times that morning and then I went back to bed, healed. I slept peacefully until it was time to get up.

It gives me great pleasure to share with you what God showed me on receiving healing from emotional wounds.

The Steps to Emotional Healing

1.   Pray. Talk to God honestly, holding nothing back. Ask Him to heal you completely, from the inside out.

This is the confidence we have in approaching God: that if we ask anything according to his will, he hears us. And if we know that he hears us – whatever we ask – we know that we have what we asked of him. 1 John 5:14, 15, NIV

2.   Stop rehearsing the negative memories! Stop playing them over again and again in your mind. We have trouble forgetting past hurts because we keep rehearsing them, so we have to stop rehearsing them. Consider this: We rehearse phone numbers so we won't forget them; we rehearse materials for a test so that we won't forget it. If we keep rehearsing negative memories, we won't forget them either.

Finally, brothers, whatever is true, whatever is noble, whatever is right, whatever is   admirable – if   anything   is   excellent   or praiseworthy – think about such things. Philippians 4:8, NIV

3.   Create a picture of yourself healed and of the wounded relationship healed. Begin to speak as if that picture were true, as if the healing has already taken place. If you are still too wounded to form a picture of a healed relationship, ask God to give you a picture of the relationship healed. (*For it is God who works in you to will and to act according to his good pleasure. Philippians 2:13, NIV*

Begin to say how you want to be and how you want the relationship to be. Begin to speak positive words, and think positive thoughts about the person or the relationship, instead of rehearsing the past hurts.

4.   Trust God to do what He says that He will do.

This is the confidence that we have in approaching God: that if we ask anything according to his will, he hears us. And if we know that he hears us – whatever we ask – we know that we have what we asked of him. 1 John 5:14, 15, NIV

Trust in the Lord with all your heart and lean not on your own understanding. In all your ways acknowledge him and he will direct your paths Proverbs 3:5, 6 NIV

5.   Be practical, and take baby steps in restoring the relationship.

A man's heart devises his way, but the Lord directs his steps. Proverbs 16:9, KJV.

The Journey Completed

I was so hungry to be healed that I wrote down these five steps for receiving emotional healing and I followed them exactly as God, through the Holy Spirit, gave them to me.

I prayed, earnestly and sincerely. I stopped rehearsing the painful memories. I replaced the negative thoughts with a picture of a loving relationship between me and my family member *(this was really hard, so I had to ask God to give me a picture of a healed, loving relationship)*. I trusted God to direct my paths. I took very small steps *(I mean little bitty steps)* in welcoming that person back into my life. We are better. I am healed.

My journey to really understanding how to be healed from emotional wounds took 12 years. But now I know how to receive and keep true emotional healing, from the inside out. I know how to take off the sackcloth of mourning so that God can break alive in me with His peace and healing power.

Starting Over
by Elaine B. Johnson

Though we are slaves, our God has not deserted us in
our bondage. He has shown us kindness... He has
granted us new life to rebuild...
Ezra 9:9 (NIV)

I was so happy! I had met the man of my dreams and was getting married. The wedding was beautiful. We honeymooned in Madrid, Spain.

We drove a Mercedes Benz, owned an apartment building in Chicago and a cattle ranch in Texas. I had a Master's degree, was active in my church, had a job, and brought home a paycheck and I was beaten. I was beaten whenever, "I did something that 'upset' my husband."

"Upsetting my husband" could be anything from talking on the telephone, not washing the dishes, visiting my mother, spending time with his parents, not having dinner ready when he wanted it, not agreeing with him...the list could go on and on.

I remember one time we were in Texas and I had spent the day with his parents. When I returned home, he threw a shoe at me, which hit me on the head. The injury required seven stitches.

On another occasion he pushed me, knocked me around, and I fell and broke my finger. Another time he pushed me, kicked me, threw me down and pulled out his pocketknife, put it to my throat and said that he would cut it.

Many days I went to work with a bruised face that I tried to cover up with makeup. Today I know that you never really cover it up. Family and friends just try not to notice. I have been told that it broke my mother's heart, but she always said, "When Elaine has had enough, she will leave."

I lived with abuse for 14 years. I really believed in my marriage vows, "for better or worse." I prayed constantly for my husband. I asked the Lord to change my husband or change me. Many times he would say to me, "If you leave me, I'll kill you and your family." Then at other times he'd say, "If you don't like it just leave."

One day after my mother's death, we had an argument and he said, "If you don't like it just leave." I packed a suitcase and a shopping bag and left. I left the car, the furniture, the building, the ranch—I left all the things because they were no longer important to me.

I filed for divorce, and three years later I was granted a divorce, with a reasonable divorce settlement.

A year or so after our divorce, my former husband was killed with a broken neck in a head-on automobile accident on an expressway that I can see from my living room window. Even though we were divorced, I was the one who claimed his body, picked out the clothing for his funeral, and shipped his body back to Texas for the burial. All of my things that were not granted to me in the divorce settlement were made available to me.

God kept me through all the years. God showed me that sometimes getting the better in a situation means leaving and starting a new life. He showed me that if you trust in Him, He will take care of every situation. Like Job, my last

years have become my best years. I will continue to serve
Him as long as I live.

  # The Hand of God

For all this I considered in my heart even to declare all
this, that the righteous, and the wise, and their works,
are in the hand of God:
Ecclesiastes 9:1 (KJV)

On March 4, 1961 a tornado ravaged the South side of
Chicago at about 1 p.m. that afternoon. Radio reports
indicated a "tornado watch." I was an instructor for the
Illinois Bell Telephone Company and my students and I
watched a dull cloud cover the window of the office. Shortly
thereafter, we received a call from the downtown
headquarters giving permission to close the office and all
employees were dismissed for the day.

As I drove west on 83rd Street near Stony Island in my 88
Oldsmobile, off in the distance I saw what appeared to be a
very dark "something." All of a sudden, the "something"
got closer and I could see dust and debris whirling right for
me. My car began to shake, I pressed down harder on the
brake pedal because the wind was so strong that this 8-
cylinder car engine could not force the car to move forward.
My only thought was to try to get home safely.

In a split second, this three-ton automobile had been picked
up and sat down in a ditch. Looking around me, total panic
set in. I jumped out of the car with the engine running,

windshield wipers going and my purse on the seat.   I
climbed out of this shallow ditch and ran towards the first
building which was a small service station that sat about
fifty yards from the corner. As I ran into the station, several
people witnessed my car being moved sideways into the
ditch. I was hysterical and they tried to calm me down by
shaking me, slapping me and offering me a cold can of 7-
Up. When I gained my composure the tornado had passed
and dissipated into Lake Michigan. The men took their tow
truck and led the car back upon the street and sent me on
my way home.

It was not to be a direct trip. Downed electrical wires;
uprooted trees; pieces of roofs and similar debris covered
the street. I maneuvered my way west in a maze—first on
83rd street, then 79th, 87th, 95th, and back to 81st street. Two
hours later I finally arrived home. I pulled into the garage
making sure I left enough space for my husband to pull in
when he arrived home. After saying my prayers for the
third time since leaving my office, I prepared dinner for my
family and watched the reports on the devastation and
destruction the tornado had left in its wake. A few minutes
later my husband came in and asked "What happened to the
car?"

After I related my experience of that day, we went into the
garage and there sat my 88 Oldsmobile on four flat tires. I
know my guardian angel was with me that day and about
ten years later a near death experience in the hospital
confirmed this. Throughout my life I've been protected by
the "hand of God," that guides my daily life.

Taking a Stand for Righteousness and Justice

For the Lord takes delight in his people;
he crowns the humble with salvation...
to carry out the sentence written against them.
Psalm 149: 4, 9

We pull for the underdog. We love it when the horse far back in the field comes charging down the stretch to win.

God pulls for the underdog too. The psalmist should praise for the humble and takes pleasure in the faithful ones. Faithfulness and humility are real winners.

In this journey of life, God does not call us to be successful, but God calls us to be faithful and God remains faithful to us.

David, the writer of many psalms, can most appreciate this expectation. Though David failed at times in his ethics, integrity, and morality, he maintained his fidelity to Yahweh. Aside from his flings with lust and power, he never worshipped or allowed the worship of other gods and for this reason was considered to be a faithful king.

A common New Testament word for sin is hamartia, which literally means "missing the mark." We cannot hit the target all of the time. The basketball player does well to shoot fifty percent. The baseball player who hits successfully one-third of the time is doing well. But the reality of failure doesn't keep these athletes from making the attempt, and therefore, from succeeding.

Do we try to do God's will? Do we attempt to place ourselves in the arena of God's influence called "the means of grace" (such as worship, prayer, study, scripture reading, tithing, fasting, the sacraments, serving the poor and marginalized)?   To try and then fail is simply human. Failing to try is denial of God's will and love.

We are forever the underdogs, because we will never "get it right." We will stay on the journey, by giving it our best. And best of all: God is on our side.

Taking a stand for the underdog may not be a popular stand. But if we recall the life of Jesus—He always was for the underdog, helping those who had a need. Need comes in many fashions and styles. There are times when the need may be food, clothing, shelter and other physical items. Then a need may come forth in a moral form and a form for righteousness and justice to prevail.

When I was a classroom teacher in the school system of Chicago, I was teaching at a school where 41 teachers were employed. There was one Black teacher who the principal had a problem with his teaching Black History. When the time came for students to perform in a singing assembly, the principal wanted his class to sing "Old Dixie." He refused to teach "Old Dixie" because of the slave connotation. She set out to get a committee of teachers to prepare 10 charges against the teacher in question. It so happened that I had to keep the students of the teacher who taught in the next room from me. When the committee meeting was over, I asked what the meeting was about. The teacher whose classroom was next to mine informed me of the 10 charges they had to draw up with the intention of presenting them the next morning at a faculty meeting which included community members and parents. When I learned this, I informed the teacher against whom the charges would be presented. He phoned the parents of his students and prepared himself for the next day's meeting.

As the meeting began, one of the committee members began reading the charges. She read the first, then the second and started on the third charge. I heard a voice speak to my conscience and say, if you sit here and say nothing you are condoning this wrong against your fellow teacher who is the underdog. I raised my hand to speak. I spoke on Board of Education policy where the evaluation and reprimanding charges were not to come from colleagues, but it was the responsibility of the principal. I spoke to the fact that the entire matter was out of order in the setting in which we were involved. When I finished my speech, the principal announced the close of the meeting and hand claps of joy came from those all around the room

After the meeting I just knew this principal would find a way to fire me, but instead she offered me a promotion. God has come to my rescue over and over again. When we have the courage to stand up for a just cause, God will take care of us.

Listening to our Elders

Lord Make a Way!

***I will say of the LORD, He is my refuge and my
fortress: my God; in him will I trust.
Psalm 91:1-2 (KJV)***

I was born the middle child of three children around the
turn of the century. Since my older brother didn't wish to
be bothered with my long name, Sister is the name he gave
me. He was three years older than me and my younger
sister was two years younger than me. We started out a
happy family of five living in a Southern city. Papa was a
chief cook at resort hotels in neighboring cities.

Our happy life soon turned tragic when Papa took to
alcohol, which at that time caused many families to suffer.
Not only did alcohol stretch out its wicked prong, but that
of another woman crushed the spirits of Mama. The struggle
to care for her three young children in the midst of dealing
with a wayward husband was too much for her to bear.
While she had a great deal of pride and self-respect, she had
few, if any, earthly friends to talk to. Her battle was
detrimental to her and her family. She committed suicide by
the use of her husband's razorblade. While she laid in the
backyard with a white sheet as a cover, we stood in the
doorway. My brother held my younger sister in his arms
while I stood beside him. None of us was quite old enough
to realize what had happened.

After Mama's death, our sense of family changed forever.
We were separated. Both my brother and sister were
fortunate enough to find good homes and I only saw my
sister once again, about ten years later. Sadly no one seemed
to want me. My father was working as a cook at a resort

hotel in another city, so I was sent to live with my father's brother's wife, and my life wasn't pleasant in the least.

Aunt Em lived in a boxy house and worked for a white family who lived across the street. Still not yet three years of age, Aunt Em left me in that boxy house alone all day without any heat during the winter months. When she returned from her day work, she found me, a wet, nasty brat and I was punished for being in my helpless state. There was very little, if anything that I could do for myself at that age. The punishment was administered for several days.

I remember another boxy house next door to Aunt Em's. In the family of that home, there were two sisters who were most likely teenagers. They would come in, dress me and play with me at times. On one particular afternoon both me and my bed were in a mess. I was carried outside, naked, and placed in a tub of water. While being washed off, a piece of secretion was placed in my mouth, with the command, "Eat this." I would not eat it, but I howled and sputtered as the girls laughed with glee. After this incident I was removed from Aunt Em's. The bad treatment was forgiven in later years, but not forgotten.

I went to live with my father for a little while where I was fortunate enough to have a playmate. I remember a big yard with green grass and a large tree, which stood near the well. Other children from the neighborhood came to play which was nice. The best part of all was that I got to see my father frequently, but unfortunately this was short-lived.

One bright, sunny day while the other children and I were out playing, a pretty lady came along and watched us for a while. She called out to me and we chatted briefly. A few days later I went to live with her in a big, pretty two-story house.

We lived in the upper story of the house. I liked my new home at first, but something went wrong. I was not allowed to go outside and play with the children who lived in the backyard of this home. For days I sat on a *Brown Mule Chewing Tobacco* box, looking out of an upstairs window down into the town. This was very monotonous for a three-year-old who wanted to go outside and play. Whenever I would seek permission to play, I was always given a flat denial of "No," which made me cry. This would result in a beating and oftentimes I would be thrown into a little dark closet. I was further tormented when my guardians would knock on the door and tell me, "The old Boogerman is going to get you."

In those days there was no running water in the best of homes. The drinking water came from wells and you attended to personal necessities by using a little out-house commonly called the *Garden House*. This was my way of getting off that *Brown Mule Chewing Tobacco Box* and out of that upstairs room.

Whenever I would pass the downstairs resident on my way to the *Garden House* I often found her sitting with a little basket in her lap mending soaks. She was a lovable person called "Nin" by everyone. Whenever I passed through, I would fall on my knees and say, "Nin, take me to be your little girl. I'll be your nice pretty little girl." I would then run out to the *Garden House*, stay a little while and run back upstairs only to be scolded or beaten and accused of stopping in the kitchen to steal food, which was not true. Oftentimes I was met on the back stoop where the well was located. There on a table sat a pail of water, a dipper, and a tin basin used to wash your face and hands. After being falsely accused and telling the truth, I received a blow to my face. As usual, tears rolled down my face while I was being yelled at. The basin was filled with water and I was commanded to wash my face. As I bent over to do as I was commanded, my head would be held down in the pan of water. I was then marched upstairs only to sit on the *Brown Mule* box for the rest of the day.

This treatment was a bit more than Nin could stand. One day she confronted my guardian and demanded that she never hit or abuse me again. "She's my child and I'll do what I want," was the reply. With this remark, rage boiled forth in my guardian and down my head went into the basin. On this particular day Nin grabbed my guardian's hand, threw her off the porch, into the backyard and then went to beat her up. On observation, the white neighbor above, and the black neighbor below were standing out grinning while watching the affray. Nin became ashamed, went back into her room and took me with her. Later when my guardian's husband came home, Nin explained what happened and suggested that they move away from the home. He was apologetic and said it was against his will in the beginning and the mistreatment of children was his wife's weakness. I spent the night and next morning with my guardians and the following afternoon my father came, took me upon his lap and talked to Nin about adopting me, which did come to pass. From that day forward I was happy, and for once felt loved.

Nin and her husband had taken on the responsibility of a little three-year-old homeless, almost parentless child. They had two grown sons and had raised two other children who at that time were grown and out in life for themselves.

I grew up happy and healthy in Nin's home. I was able to play with other children and made several friends at school. When I was fifteen and in the ninth grade I was able to substitute teach for a week when the fifth grade teacher went home for a week to attend her mother's funeral. I was paid $15.00 for my work, and I was happy of course.

After graduation from school, I found myself without any plans. Three of my classmates were going to Hampton Institute and working their way through school. I asked Nin if I could go to Hampton with them and she said, "No Sister."

I spent the summer helping with the washing and ironing of white folks' clothes, but I kept praying for the Lord to open up a way for me. One Monday morning while I was standing in the back of Nin's house in my bare feet rubbing on white folks clothes, I continuously prayed, "Lord, make a way." Suddenly I heard the clumping of horses feet, which ended in Nin's backyard and stopped near where I was washing. When our pastor stepped out of the buggy, I was greatly embarrassed but courteous in my conversation.

"Hello Sister, how are you?" the Pastor asked.

"Fine, Reverend," I replied. "Please excuse the way I look"

He smiled then said, "You're all right. Are you going to school this fall?"

"No Sir, but I would love to go."

"Where do you wish to go?"

"I want to go to Shaw University."
The pastor chuckled to himself and after talking with Nin, he informed me that I may indeed have the opportunity to go to college. The following week I met with the Dean of Shaw University for a scholarship. This was in 1916. I assured the Dean that I could make it in the First Year Class

and was given a scholarship of $4.00 per month. I waited on student tables for $4.00 per month and Nin washed and ironed and sent me $4.00 per month. Can you imagine now going to college for $12.00 per month?

While a student at Shaw I had a dream about my sister during the Flu Epidemic of 1918. In the dream, my sister and I were out for a walk when we came up on a fence with a gate. On the other side was the most beautiful flower garden we had ever seen. We both remarked about the beauty of the garden. My sister opened the gate and went into the garden. As she entered, she said, "Goodbye Sister. I must leave you now." At the time I didn't understand what the dream meant, but Nin informed me a month later that my sister had passed.

I walked out of Shaw University in 1920 with three certificates and started a teaching career of close to 50 years. I also got married in a big church wedding and moved to another city. I received many honors for my classroom activities, and retired in June of 1966.

As I sit and take a photographic picture of my life, I am thankful to my Heavenly Father and His untiring hand for leading me thus far. There were low roads and high roads. Crooked and narrow paths, which broadened as I walked along. But with a good Christian foster mother, His word and some good Christian leadership, I was able to pull through.

There were reasons why I should have hated and been resentful. Instead, I accepted love, peace, joy and prayer. They have paid off. The Lord has taken care of me thus far and I thank Him almost every day and almost every hour for His love and care.

People often ask me, "What is your secret for such a long life?"

I put God first and read my Bible daily.

I trust Him.

I treat everyone as I like to be treated.

My Soul Looks Back
by Hallie B. Hendrieth-Smith

Now I am about to go the way of all the earth. You know with all your heart and soul that not one of all the good promises the LORD your God gave you has failed. Every promise has been fulfilled; not one has failed.
Joshua 23:14 (NIV)

"How I Got Over." My soul looks back and praises God. This statement comes from a Negro spiritual that I learned early in my life. I paraphrased it to express my feelings. The title of the spiritual is "How I Got Over, My Soul Looks Back and Wonders." Being the positive person that my parents taught me to be, I praise God and thank my parents for where I am today.

I was born in Alabama and reared in a two-parent family along with my four sisters and three brothers. My education began in a one-room schoolhouse that was provided by the church in a segregated community. At that time there were no public schools for African American children. My mother and the women of the church were the teachers. My father and the men of the church supplied the fuel for the "pot belly" stove with logs they cut from the trees that grew near the church. We were inspired to read although the books and magazines were the "throwaways" from the white schools since African Americans were not permitted to use the public library. If you knew someone who worked in the library, you could get a book occasionally.

After I completed the fourth grade, I entered the first junior high school that was built for African American children in that community. The school was named for one of the teachers who had finished Knoxville College and returned to teach in our community. I recall the excitement. We finally had a school building with rooms and teachers who had graduated from college. These teachers were sent to colleges that were supported by Christian denominations that provided schools for African American children. Had it not been for those private schools, we would not have had the opportunities to get an education. These teachers exposed us to music, drama, art, math and science. Bible and Home Economics were taught daily.

Growing up in the deep South was a "bittersweet" experience. Private schools for African Americans placed an "educational" shield around me. Yes, I walked to school or rode in the wagon with all of the children in the community that my father's wagon could accommodate when it rained. My father was the guardian angel in our community. When the water rose in the pond in front of our house, he carried us across on his shoulders. When it rained he drove us in the wagon.

I remember the two mules, Bob and Mattie, who were pulling the wagon. My father taught us a lesson on taking responsibility using the mules as an example. Bob was lazy and did not always pull his share of the load. My father hitched him up shorter than Mattie. He explained that was his method of forcing Bob to share in his responsibility.

I praise God daily for my parents. They explained segregation to us in a way that we felt sorry for the practice all around us. They told us that people who practiced discrimination were ignorant of the blessings of God. When we saw the "colored" signs over the water fountains or the "this way colored" signs, I remember that my parents told us, "You are special. God don't make junk." We were encouraged to drink water before we left home and use the bathroom. Although we did not have running water or toilet paper we were taught to be proud and look forward to the future when there would be changes. I did not know what they meant at that time, but here are some of the daily things we did to "get over," during that difficult time.

We had to wash our clothing in a tub using a rub board.

We had to pump water from a pump that my father installed, or draw it from the well in our yard.

We were taught to make soap.

We used coals to heat the irons to iron our clothing.

The farm my father had was taken from him when we were small. He kept his truck farm and his syrup mill. These were the only economic provisions he had to feed his family. My mother washed and ironed shirts for the doctors in the local hospital and cooked for one of the judges in town. We were taught to iron shirts and cook when we were young. We did not have electricity so we studied by firelight.

My parents taught us to believe in ourselves. If anyone can "you can" was a daily phrase in our household. No one can keep you from reaching your goal unless you fail to set one.

"Life for Me Ain't Been No Crystal Stair," (Langston Hughes).

I walked to town to keep from sitting in the back of the bus.

I learned to cook to keep from going in the back of the restaurants.

I learned to sew so as to style the hand me down clothing from whites.

I learned to wash and iron clothes from white families to keep from babysitting.

I sat by the fireside many nights studying so I could make good grades.

My heart was set on teaching from the time I was a small child. When I finished high school, I took the State Board of Examination to qualify for a provisional license. This was possible for we could only teach African American children. Schools were in session for only five months each year due to the need for African American farm labor. I took advantage of the time when school was out to complete my education. I earned my B.A. degree from Alabama State University.

My first opportunity to teach was in Tilden, Alabama. This was a school for children who had not been of the plantation where the school was located. After two years, I was hired to teach at Selma University's middle school. My first check was $25.00 monthly, later $100.00. Teachers worked in the cafeteria during lunch and the proceeds from the lunchroom and contributions from the State Baptist Convention were used to pay the teachers. This was a wonderful experience for me because it gave me an opportunity to demonstrate my strong commitment to help children. I was so passionate about my job and for student learning that I would have worked for free.

When I moved to the Midwest I thought I was in the Promised Land, but I soon discovered that I was a long way from that.

Schools were segregated.

African-American children were placed in Special Education classes.

Students in regular classes weren't challenged.

Children were poor readers, had little knowledge of their history and had low self-esteem.

I was one of nine African American teachers hired to integrate the schools. I cannot begin to list all of the problems we encountered during integration. We made it by trusting in God and praying daily for strength to hold on. I am happy to say that the African American church, which I classify as the "Cornerstone of African American Culture," provided the stamina that helped to get over. Yes, I have been blessed to complete a Master's degree and a Specialist degree. I look back over my life and I say I have a testimony God brought me through.

Wait on the Lord
by Betty L. Hyter

Wait on the Lord: be of good courage, and He
shall strengthen thine heart: wait, I say, on the Lord
Psalms 27:14 (KJV)

I was the ninth child in a family of eleven children born to beautiful parents in a small town in Alabama. My school was approximately 3 ½ to 4 miles from my farmhouse and we walked to school and back each day. Since we did not own a car we walked everywhere we went, unless my father hired a neighbor to take us necessary places that were too far to walk.

My father was a Primitive Baptist preacher as well as a farmer. We lived on the family farm that had been passed down from generation to generation. Whereas our farm did not produce huge gains, we were still happy just knowing that we were independent, tilling our own land rather than a plantation owner's land. From today's standard, we were poverty stricken, but we were unaware of the status. We had lots of love, probably lots of problems that we as children were unaware of and lots of everything but money. Most of all, we had lots of faith. Church was a must every week and sometimes twice on Sunday. Services were long and as children we had no Junior Church so we attended Sunday School and joined our parents or a relative for church service. Aside from a lot of shouting by some of the members and what they called "good" praying, we seldom understood what the preacher was trying to get across. Maybe I was partial, but I always enjoyed my father's preaching. I was so proud of him!

My Dad was Baptist and my mother was Methodist (CME). The church services were quite different, the Methodists were quiet spoken, the songs were beautiful hymns and the members seldom, if ever, got emotional enough to shout. The Baptist preachers, on the other hand, did a lot of whooping, the singing was non-hymnal, there was a lot of moaning in the songs, and the service was very long.

We attended the local Baptist church on the first and third Sunday and the Methodist church on the second and fourth Sunday. The Methodist church was closer to home than my father's church, therefore it was convenient for my mother to remain in her home church.

After we grew up and transportation had gotten better, my mother joined where her heart was all along—my father's church. The one thing that was universal in our community was that everything you did or said was centered on the Bible. Parents would discipline their children and give them directions Biblically, saying things such as: "Do not take the Lord's name in vain," "Do unto others as you would have them do unto you," and the list goes on. This type of upbringing became a part of me and as a result, even as a child, I was pretty grounded in the Lord's way, aware of what prayer could do and had a great appreciation for what was right and what was wrong.

This Biblical way of life with our parents, more from action than from reading gave me a sense of faith and a love for the Lord. I learned to pray early in life and my prayers have blessed me. As a child, long before I was dating age, I prayed that the Lord would give me a good husband and He did. I have had 47 years of that blessing.

Whenever trials came during my upbringing and my adult life, I felt that the strength I acquired from the way my parents nurtured me physically, emotionally, and spiritually has rewarded me immensely in handling difficult situations. I do not rely totally on my parent's directions, for both of them have gone on to heaven. I try to continue their legacy by knowing the Lord for myself so I can affect my children, and so that they can affect their children and the legacy continues. My mother was my role model as a parent. I used to tell her that I hope I can be half as successful in bringing up my children as she was with her children. She always expressed that if you do right, right will follow you. That was ingrained in me as a child. I want to live the way He wants me to live, to please Him and as a result He will bless me tremendously. This is my first key to how I got over.

When I was 14, my parents moved to the city of Huntsville, Alabama and to a much better house than our farmhouse. After about 15 years, the farmhouse was sold and my parents built a beautiful home in the suburbs. Psalm 27:14 continues to reign doesn't it? Just as I experienced the Lord bringing us through at home with my parents, my husband and I have had similar experiences of the Lord's hand helping us through.

My husband and I were married November 13, 1954 after a courtship of about five years. He was a college senior in Alabama and I was a Nursing student in Atlanta who decided to change her career from Nursing to Marriage. While he attended college, we both worked. I was a Nurse's Aide in a local hospital and he worked part-time in a bakery, as a brick mason in the summer and whatever he could find to do, he carried a full load in college.

He graduated in 1956 with a degree in Biology. He taught school one year in Alabama and the following year we moved to Detroit with our six-month-old son while we lived temporarily with my sister. We only intended to stay for the summer while my husband worked on his Master's degree. He worked for Ford Motor Company and went to school part-time. At the end of the summer we decided to stay in Detroit because his salary there was better than the teaching salary back at home. The fact that he could continue his graduate studies was an added bonus.

He went on to work in the school system for 35 years as a science teacher. After teaching in Detroit for seven years, the Lord blessed him with a National Science Foundation Fellowship at Cornell University and our family had grown by three. The six of us went to Ithaca, New York and faced challenges. There was a lot of competition at Cornell; my husband had to study very hard. With many hours of hard work, sleepless nights, prayer and an extra summer he was able to get his Master's. Financial support came from his stipend and I worked one night a week at a Nursing Home to help with the finances. I think I made $10.00 per night (good laundry money).

My husband completed his Masters in 1963 and we returned to Detroit. Once again we lived temporarily with my sister and we thanked God for her, her husband and their hospitality. After a few days we found an upstairs apartment. We were on our way to a one-bedroom apartment in an old dilapidated apartment building when we saw this upstairs flat for rent. We inquired about it and were able to rent the flat. What a blessing this was because it gave us two bedrooms instead of one and more space for myself, my husband, and our four children.

Leroy returned to the Board of Education as head of a Science Department at a high school. In 1964 we got a double blessing. We were blessed with another daughter, and we were able to buy a beautiful colonial home with three bedrooms and a full basement. We lived in this home until 1974 when we moved to our present home. Once again, Psalm 27:14 reigns.

We now have five beautiful children and my husband later became the supervisor of all of the high school science departments for the Detroit Public School System. Between the births of our children, my working part-time as a Nurse's Aide and later an LPN, I attended college and received my B.A. in Sociology. For 21 years I worked as a Social Worker for the state of Michigan. We raised our children and sent them to college. Our reward of sacrifice has been high. Our children have made us nothing but happy. There were times when the going got rough, but my husband and I came to the marriage with the same type of determination to achieve a goal, we both had a good faith foundation to pull from and we praise the Lord everyday for getting us over.

"How We Got Over" is a good question to think about. As I've pondered this question, I can say my help comes from the Lord. We accepted Him as our personal Savior. He provided: the Christian environment in which my husband and I were raised, the work ethic we received before we left home, our loving and helpful family, encouragement from family and friends, our church — past and present — for spiritual guidance, our trust in the Lord — that never faltered, our faith, our love for the Lord and the love we have for each other and for our children.

When I was eleven years old, I was excited one day over all of the dresses I received and I asked my mother to explain the increase. She answered me by reciting Matthew 6:33. That scripture has been with me ever since; my life has been based on it.

*But seek ye first the kingdom of God and His
righteousness; and all these things shall be added unto
you.*
Matthew 6:33

This is the key to how we got over.

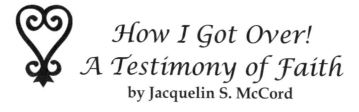

How I Got Over!
A Testimony of Faith
by Jacquelin S. McCord

*Therefore I say to you, do not worry about your
life...Look at the birds of the air, for they neither sow
nor reap nor gather into barns; yet your heavenly
Father feeds them. Are you not more value than
they?...For your heavenly Father knows that you need
all these things.*
Matthew 6:25-32 KJV

Once our two daughters were born, I knew that I wanted to
be a stay-at-home mom. I figured God did not entrust me
with two of His angels to let someone else raise them.
During a time when my peers were trying to figure out how
to break the glass ceiling, I was trying to figure out how to
finagle our one-income family budget, determined that with
the help of God, we would manage. I saved coupons for
grocery shopping and made most of our clothing.
Household furnishings were gifts or bought from thrift
shops. I did my own version of pre-school home schooling

and took advantage of many of our community resources. We often visited the public library, one of our favorite places. I enrolled the girls in the YWCA programs where they learned tap and ballet dancing and took swimming lessons. By the time they were four years old they were jumping off the diving board into nine feet of water. The city parks had great classes, including tennis, track and winter sports. The churches we attended in New York and Chicago provided many opportunities for our children's spiritual and educational growth. We had everything we needed, and a great deal more. In fact, people thought we "had money!"

And when He had taken the five loaves and the two fish, he looked up to heaven, blessed and broke the loaves, and gave them to His disciples to set before them...So they all ate and were filled...Now those who had eaten the loaves were about five thousand men. Mark 6: 41, 42

The way God multiplied our income is a modern-day example of the story of the five loaves of bread and two fish, especially when it came to the education of our children. In addition to staying home, I also wanted what I considered to be the best education for them even though my husband's salary was barely enough for one adult. To support two adults, two children, and private school education for them appeared unthinkable. I had heard about private schools from some of the other mothers, but knew nothing about them. Although I knew a bit about Catholic schools, my husband and I were products of working-class families and public schools. Growing up, we didn't even know private schools existed much less anyone who attended them. We knew no one with connections to these schools who might "get us in" (which we thought was needed).

While we were in New York, I heard about a great kindergarten program at Sarah Lawrence College in nearby

Bronxville. Sarah Lawrence was at that time an all women's college and the most expensive college in the United States. Its early childhood education program was founded by Dr. Stone, who had written a book considered to be the "Bible" in early childhood education. Although he was now dead, his wife carried on his work as the director of the Early Childhood Center. The first problem was tuition and the second, transportation. To get my daughter to the school, I thought we would need another car. Undaunted by these problems, I called Mrs. Stone and arranged to visit the school, which was everything I had hoped for. I liked the child-centered philosophy and the caring staff. We had our daughter tested and the school accepted our application. We were able to make the initial payment on the tuition. The school put me in touch with another mother who lived three blocks from us and we agreed to car pool. By the grace of God, the money was there, the school gave us a partial scholarship, and we paid the rest.

But the blessings didn't stop there. Although she could have stayed at Sarah Lawrence for first grade, we needed to find another school afterward. Other mothers were talking about an Ethical Cultural School called Fieldston in the Bronx, another private school located off the beaten path. In all likelihood, if you didn't know about the school, you wouldn't find out about it. Fieldston was the most expensive of the three schools I learned about. The first school I visited was okay, but I was not impressed. The second school was a little better, but we knew few of the children who attended the school. I went to Fieldston just to see what it was like. My heart sank, because I loved the school and I knew we couldn't afford it. The school was perfect for what I wanted in education for my children: child-friendly, hands-on, small, family-friendly and on and on. Fieldston went from pre-kindergarten through high

school. Once a child was enrolled there, we wouldn't have
to look for another school until college.

As it turns out, the school loved us too. They helped
navigate the application process and encouraged us to
apply. Our daughter would have to take a series of tests
with an independent testing agency, which cost several
hundred dollars. They waived the fees for us. She did quite
well on the tests and was admitted to the school. The
wonderful thing about this process was, if one child in the
family attends the school subsequent siblings are
automatically admitted. We were given scholarships and
waivers and struggled through to pay our portion. There
was no bus service for the students, but we again arranged
carpooling with other parents.

When our daughters were in the third grade and
kindergarten, my husband was offered a job with the
University of Chicago, which had a school from pre-
kindergarten through high school listed among the top 25
schools in the country. Again our daughters could go there
through high school. We flew to Chicago to see if this new
opportunity was worth uprooting our family. Chicago was
a city we knew little about, a place in which we had no
family or friends—just each other and God. After our visit
to Chicago, we discussed over and over again the pros and
cons and then decided to move.

We liked the Lab School and the education our daughters
would get there. We were given a substantial discount on
the tuition because my husband was an employee of the
university. Even after he left the university, we were able to
reduce cost of tuition through scholarships. Both daughters
graduated from high school having received an excellent
education. The older one was an accomplished flutist, spoke
French and Spanish fluently, did ballet, ran track, and had

the lead part in Shakespeare's Mid-Summer Night's Dream in her senior year. The younger was an accomplished vocalist, played the piano, had a working knowledge of German and Spanish, did African and Jazz dancing, and was co-captain of the girls' basketball team.

Do you not know that those who run in a race all run, but one receives the prize? Run in such a way that you may obtain it.
I Corinthians 9:24

College would be the next challenge before us. We had promised each of the girls that we would support their choice in college and prayed that they would make wise decisions. Our older daughter chose Columbia University's Barnard College, an all women's college in New York City. Our younger daughter chose to attend the University of Michigan in Ann Arbor.

Again we saw God's blessings on our family. My mother-in-law was from West Virginia and at that time lived in California. A friend of hers, who still lived in West Virginia, published a newspaper which covered Charleston and its surroundings. Residents and former residents subscribed to the paper because it kept them posted on what was going on back home. Mom McCord wrote to her friend and told her that her granddaughter was going to attend the University of Michigan. She ran an article about it in the newspaper. A former resident of West Virginia and subscriber of the newspaper saw the story and called my mother-in-law to tell her that she and her husband lived fifteen minutes from the school and to invite us to come and visit her when we came up there. We did and they gave us a key to their apartment. Whenever we went to Ann Arbor we stayed with them. When our daughter was sick during the four years she attended the university, they took care of her.

But the blessings didn't stop there! Daughter number one decided she wanted to go to law school. Then she decided she wanted to earn a Master's in Business Administration as well. She was accepted into Northwestern University's JD/MBA. As God would have it, she got into Northwestern University Law School on a full scholarship that covered her tuition and living expenses. She finished the four-year program in three and a half years, graduated with honors, and traveled throughout Europe during what would have been her last semester.

Daughter number two decided to go to graduate school to get her Master's in Business Administration and was blessed with a scholarship to attend the University of Southern California.

I share this brief account about the education of my daughters in an attempt to give inspiration and hope to the readers. Perhaps you are like me and want to stay at home and raise your children. Or maybe you have a dream deferred and are wondering how you are going to make it. May you be encouraged to follow your heart, the dream that God has given you; allow Him to make the provisions for it to manifest.

However, I don't want to leave you with the impression that our lives were a bed of ease, because they weren't. We certainly had our share of tears, disappointments and frustrations. We worked hard and made many sacrifices, there was much we endured and many things we went without. We were not however, just sponges who soaked up our blessings and never did anything to bless others in return. There is real joy when you can take what God has given you and share it with others. When my daughters were little, I started an infant nursery at my church, allowing parents the freedom to enjoy the worship service with the knowledge that their children were well taken care of. I often served as room mother and parent volunteer at the girls' schools, and as a Girl Scout troop leader. My husband and I served boards and organizations that helped to raise money to and promote education for children.

My daughters also used their talents and skills to share their blessings with others. During their high school years, they were tutors in an after-school program for elementary students. In college, they worked in the work-study program. One worked as the manager of the cafeteria in her dorm and the other was the director of a hostess program. They both volunteered as mentors and tutors for children in the juvenile detention center.

I am proud to say that our daughters are beautiful, well-educated, Christian young women who have not forgotten how they got over.

Afterword

The Truth Will Set You Free
by Sarah Nkele Matlhare

And you shall know the truth, and the truth shall make you free."
John 8:32 (NKJV)

Each morning I rise from my sleep and start my day with a hearty breakfast. As I look out my window while sipping my coffee I am greeted by the sad and harsh reality of my country. Each morning I watch several funeral processions pass by my home—all due to the AIDS pandemic, which is wiping out my country. As you are reading my testimony, the spread of the virus continues to escalate.

Over the past 15 years I have seen first hand the devastation and destruction caused by this pandemic in Botswana. My husband, a physician, and I, a pharmacy owner, come into contact with HIV patients on a daily basis. Due to the unavailability and expense of anti-retro viral medication the pandemic has killed tens of thousands. Thirty-six percent of the adult population in Botswana is HIV positive, and one in three children is infected as well.

The government of Botswana has launched public health campaigns through media, encouraging everyone to practice the ABCs of HIV/AIDS. Abstain, Be careful and Condomize. Yet this pandemic continues to grow and most directly affects the 15-29-year-old population. This affects our workforce and soon we will have children and elders, but not many in between those ages to sustain our economy.

In Botswana, the stigma attached to this pandemic is so strong that people don't get tested for HIV and by the time they realize they have the virus it is too late. They have infected several others and the stage of their disease has advanced to full-blown AIDS. They are afraid of the truth, but they need to realize the truth will set you free. Additionally, the pandemic affects poor communities in disproportionate numbers. The expense of the drugs is one factor that increases the likelihood of death. Due to improper nourishment and lack of a balanced diet in these communities the body's immune system isn't strong.

Thousands of children have been left behind as orphans. Botswana has 68,000 HIV/AIDS orphans in a country with a population of 1.7 million. The children are living on the street, with no home and no family who are willing to take them in, often due to the stigma associated with HIV/AIDS. I knew that something had to be done to increase awareness and provide support and supplies to those infected with and affected by HIV/AIDS in my country.

Having been a Missionary in the African Methodist Episcopal Church for over thirty years, I enlisted the help of my sisters across the globe to make a difference. In 1998 I was a speaker at a Missionary Executive Board Meeting in Indiana. When I shared the startling statistics and the sad truth of the HIV/AIDS pandemic in Botswana, Dr. M. Joan Cousin stepped up and asked, "How can we help?"

We had undeveloped acreage and a desire to build a center where women could be empowered, enhance their skills and become more aware and cognizant of their health issues. We also knew the orphans had a need as well and aspired to provide balanced meals for these children, so that their bodies would be strong. Our wishes were greater, but this was a great way to start our mission work for HIV/AIDS in Botswana.

With a very generous donation from Dr. Cousin and her husband, Bishop Philip R. Cousin, Sr., the M. Joan Cousin Empowerment Center was born in Lobatse, Botswana. The center was built in 1999 and dedicated in 2000. Two hundred and fifty orphans who were referred by the Lobatse Town Council come to our center daily. We provide tutoring, recreation and healthy meals for these children. Our hope for them is greater. Through a partnership with *Habitat for Humanity* we plan to build cluster homes for these children so that they can live life as they used to in a village. Putting them in an orphanage would be an easy answer, but would leave them feeling abandoned due to its institutional nature.

While the Botswanan Government has recently committed to providing anti-retro viral drugs to decrease the death rate, there is a fear that a misconception about the drugs will lead to further carelessness. We must create an innovative way to educate people and let them know that HIV doesn't choose one person over another, but it can happen to anyone. Individuals must make some choices and changes in their lifestyles in order for us to successfully combat this pandemic.

Yet in the midst of my mission work I remain hopeful.

I am hopeful that one day, someone will find a cure for AIDS.

About the Contributors

Reverend Anne Barton, D.D. was born in Dooley County Georgia, raised in Cincinnati OH, and currently resides in Chicago. This experienced pastor of 23 years is a widow of several years, the mother of one daughter and grandmother of one. Her favorite scripture is Romans 8:28 "...all things work together for good to them that love God, to them who are called according to His purpose."

Michelle D. Belle-Villa is an aspiring poet/author, a wife, and the mother of two sons. The former teacher resides in Virginia and is a member of Mt. Vernon Baptist Church. Life's recipe is knowing that it is a gift from God. It's our life to live and our responsibility to live life to its fullest, so love yourself so that you may freely love others.

Sallie Bolton is a native Chicagoan and a retired case manager for the State of Illinois. The mother of four children and grandmother of ten, she has been a member of Grant Memorial A.M.E. Church for over 50 years and has served in the Women's Missionary Society for 17 years. Throughout her life, she has encouraged her children and grandchildren of the need for a good education, and to put their trust in the Lord and let Him guide their paths.

Sadie Brooks, a wife and mother, lives in the Chicago area. An active member of her local Missionary Society, her favorite scripture is 1 Corinthians 13: 13. "...And now these three remain: faith, hope and love. But the greatest of these is love."

Sharon J. Brumfield is a high school health and science teacher currently living in Detroit. This native of New

Orleans is a wife and the mother of two children. She is a member of Oak Grove A.M.E. Church where she is a member of the Nancy March Women's Missionary Society and the coordinator of Women's Ministries. Sharon focuses upon strength (Isaiah 35:4) and preparation (Psalm 23) for living by faith.

Carolyn J. Burgess is a native of Columbus, Ohio, widowed after having shared 33 years of the Christian ministry with her late husband. A retired music teacher and church musician, she has given many years of service to the Women's Missionary Society, and is now focusing her efforts on directing the Commission on Christian Education at Allen Temple A.M.E. Church in Detroit, Michigan. Her spiritual strength comes from the knowledge that God is constantly at work in our lives, directing our paths and molding us into what He would have us to be.

Brett Chambers is a native Washingtonian living in Durham, NC. An instructor in Mass Communications and Education Technology, he is active in the community promoting ways to use the arts to enhance learning skills. Brett has a daughter, Arielle, who motivates him to create more opportunities for children. He believes that God is within each of us...we just have to quiet our own voice to hear His word.

Earline Clark is a native Chicagoan with a unique history of growing up in the 1930s through the 1950s on Winthrop Ave; the only residential street given to Blacks in Uptown on the north side of Chicago. Earline is a widow and retiree from the University of Chicago where she faithfully dedicated 35 years of service. Her church home is Wayman A.M.E. where she is an officer, spiritual leader and committed servant of Christ.

Naomi M. Clay is a native Chicagoan and a retired elementary school principal. The mother of two sons, grandmother to five and great grandmother to three, she has been a member of St. John A.M.E. Church in Indianapolis, IN since the mid-1930s. She has served as a steward, class leader, Sunday School teacher and a member of the Missionary Society for over 60 years. She has been a life member for over 50 years. She has always encouraged her family and friends to serve God faithfully.

Geneva B. Coleman, is a native Texan currently living in Chicago. A member of Tau Gamma Delta and the Interdenominational Minister's Wives, she has held several positions in the Women's Missionary Society on the local, conference branch and district levels. She is married to Dr. David C. Coleman and is a mother and grandmother.

Valerie E. Cousin, has been employed in higher education finance for the past 15 years. She has contributed to several meditation journals and writes articles for her church newsletter. Valerie is the wife of a pastor and is the proud mother of two sons ages nine and 18. Her recipe for living is to always be in a spirit of "becoming." Never stop learning and expose yourself to a myriad of opportunities. This way, when [an] opportunity meets a prepared mind, success will be inevitable!

"Eve" was born in Chicago and still resides in the Chicago area where she has been a member of her church for over 40 years. She has served as a very active officer and layperson in various organizations. After her retirement as a community college professor, Eve extended her love for travel and now works as an independent cruise/travel consultant.

Evelyn Farris is a native of Montgomery, Alabama and the daughter of a C.M.E. pastor and presiding elder. An alumna of Alabama A & M University, she is a retired school teacher. She is an active member of Coleman Chapel A.M.E. Church, Kenosha, Wisconsin where she serves on the Steward Board, Lay Organization and holds Life membership in the Women's Missionary Society. Evelyn is also a member of Delta Sigma Theta Sorority, Incorporated.

Annie Marie Ford lives in Chicago and is an active member of her local Missionary Society. Her favorite scripture is John 3:16, "For God so loved the world that He gave His only begotten Son, that whosoever believeth in him should not perish, but have everlasting life.

Pearla Owens Gholston is a graduate of Barber Scotia College and Butler University. She is a wife, mother and retired teacher from the Indianapolis Public School System. An active member of St. John A.M.E. Church (Indianapolis), her favorite scripture is "Train up a child in the way he should go and when he is old he will not depart from it." She enjoys singing, reading, traveling with her family and visiting the shut-in. She believes if she can help somebody as she passes along then her living will not be in vain, and the joy she has in her heart was not given by man and cannot be taken away by anyone.

Norma J. Gibbs the Illinois Conference Branch President of the WMS, is a resident of Saline County in Southern Illinois where she has been employed as a deputy circuit clerk for the past twenty years. She is a mother, grandmother and great grandmother. A life-long member of the A.M.E. Church, she has served the Women's Missionary Society for 27 years. Her recipe for life is "But seek ye first the kingdom of God and his righteousness and all these things shall be added unto you. " (Matthew 6:33)

Jurlene Glover is a native Chicagoan and a retired nursing assistant. She and her husband Walter are the parents of one son. Jurlene has been a member of Bethel A.M.E. church in Adrian, Michigan for 28 years where she has served in many capacities. She is currently the Lay President and Conference delegate. Jurlene has always encouraged her son to trust in the Lord.

Rachelle Guillory attended California State University, Dominguez Hills and resides in California with her two children. Rachelle is the author of *The Known Stranger*, a mystery novel that will pique the interest of its readers from start to finish, contributor to the *Women of Color Devotional Bible* and the author of *Expressions of Soul*, a collection of uplifting poetry. Her recipe for living is in poetic form: With God at your side, And as your guide, Love in your heart will reside, Peace in your life will abide, The key to abundant life, Is acquiescing to the will of Christ! "Trust in the LORD with all thine heart; and lean not unto thine own understanding. In all thy ways acknowledge him and he shall direct thy paths." (Proverbs 3:5-6)

Julia A. Hagwood was born in Evanston, Illinois, the only daughter among five sons to Dr. and Mrs. W. Frederic Fisher. The widow of William Hagwood, mother to Byron and Susan, grandmother to Jordan Burns. She has served as Connectional, District, Conference, and local WMS officer. Editor of January 2003 **WMS Book of Prayers, 1995-1999 Quadrennial Bible Study Guide, God Is** publication, and numerous Bible studies. Quadrennial and District Bible study teacher, prayer warrior, WMS life member, granddaughter of charter member of Bethel, Evanston, Illinois. Civic and community volunteer, retired Pension Analyst, United Methodist Church.

Allena Henderson, a mother and grandmother lives in Iowa. Her favorite scripture is Psalms 121:1, "I will lift up mine eyes unto the hills, from whence cometh my help. My help cometh from the Lord, which made heaven and earth."

Hallie B. Hendrieth-Smith, Ed.D. is a native of Selma, Alabama currently living in Minnesota. This lifelong educator and retired principal is a graduate of Alabama State University, Selma University, University of Minnesota and St. Mary's University. Hallie has held several positions in the Women's Missionary Society on the local, conference branch and district levels and has led several children to Christ. She and her husband Reverend Noah Smith are the proud parents of five adult children who are all educators. Hallie's recipe for living is to teach children to read which builds their self-esteem. With a foundation of strong self-esteem and Christ in their lives, the children can only grow and prosper.

Mary Fleming Hughes was educated in the Chicago Public Schools and earned a Master's degree in education and a Master's degree in social work. She has worked in higher education for several years. She is a member of Ebenezer AME Church, a Christian Education worker, Sunday School teacher, and member of the Grant Women's Missionary Society. Her interests include working with children and disadvantaged populations.

Betty Louise Hyter is a retired Social Worker who lives in Detroit, Michigan. She and her husband Leroy are the proud parents of five children and the grandparents of five. An active member of Ebenezer A.M.E. Church, she has held numerous positions in the Women's Missionary Society at the local, Conference Branch and District levels. Her article, "God's Sustaining Power in Times of an Economic Crisis" appeared in the 1993-94 PME Yearbook. Family is very important to Betty, and she teaches her children and grandchildren as she was taught, "Seek ye first the kingdom of heaven and His righteousness and all things will be added unto you."

Ruth E. James is the wife of a Pastor, the mother of three and grandmother to five. She has worked in various aspects of the Church, but her lifelong dream was to be a Missionary. She believes that we should never forget from whence we have come, stay humble and have a heart and mind to serve others.

Evelyn Jefferson is a retired educator and dedicated Christian worker. She has traveled throughout Europe and Africa representing her various church and civic involvements. A lifelong member of the Lay Organization of the A.M.E. Church and Women's Missionary Society, Evelyn has been a contributing writer to the *Christian Recorder, Voice of A.M.E. Laymen,* and *The Beacon.*

Aj D. Jemison, born in Malvern, Arkansas and raised in Tulsa, Oklahoma, began her retail career at the age of 15 and now manages regional shopping malls, presently in Tampa, Florida. She recently founded *JustAj Communications,* her motivational speaking company focusing on goal-setting for children, women and businesses. A member of Beulah Baptist Institutional Church and collector of "brown angels," Aj's recipe for living is to "envision your despair and cares as light as the feather of an angels wing. Simply let go and let God take you to the heights of your dreams."

Bettye Jenkins-Allen, Ed.D., is an educator, writer and an ardent Christian worker holding membership at Woodlawn A.M.E. Church Chicago, Illinois. She is an Illinois State Education Consultant and Connectional Editor of the WMS Magazine of the AME Church. Bettye is the mother of a son and daughter, Mr. Cedric Jenkins and Dr. Jondelle B. Jenkins-Milliner and granddaughter Francesca.

Elaine B. Johnson is a native Chicagoan and retired high school teacher. She is a member of Woodlawn A.M.E. Church and the current Chicago Conference Branch President of the Women's Missionary Society. Elaine lives each day joyfully knowing that "every good and perfect gift comes from above."

Rosalind Marie Kennedy is a native Detroiter employed by the Detroit Public School System. Married for 25 years, she is a member of Greater Quinn A.M.E. Church where she has served in the Women's Missionary Society for thirty-three years. Currently serving as Steward and Bereavement Coordinator at the church, her favorite scripture is Proverbs 4:7, "Wisdom is the principal thing; therefore get wisdom: and with all thy getting, get understanding."

Bertha Ford Keys, a native of Memphis, TN, is a retired beautician. She is the wife of a pastor, mother of two sons and two daughters, and the grandmother of seven. Having served as a missionary in the A.M.E. Church for over 40 years, Bertha has encouraged many adults and children, throughout the Fourth Episcopal District, in the work of missions.

Marjorie L. Kimbrough, author, educator, is a Phi Beta Kappa graduate of the University of California and the Interdenominational Theological Center. A frequent lecturer for business, academic and religious organizations, she has published articles on business and religious subjects, has written meditations for world wide magazines, has taught on video tape, and has published six books, *Accept No Limitations, Beyond Limitations, She Is Worthy, Everyday Miracles, Stories Between the Testaments*, and *Coffee*

Breaks of Faith. She was the 1991 Georgia Author of the Year in the area of Non-Fiction. She is married to Rev. Walter L. Kimbrough, pastor of the Cascade United Methodist Church, and is the mother of two young adult sons.

Mary F. Laws lives in Battle Creek, Michigan and is an active and ardent Missionary Worker. Her favorite scripture is Psalm 100:3, "Know ye that the LORD he is God: it is he that hath made us, and not we ourselves; we are his people, and the sheep of his pasture."

Franc Levion is a pen name for this Christian writer and clinical social worker. Throughout her life, she has been an active church member—from winning Sunday School Convention oratorical contests and serving as a Junior usher as a teenager to serving as the church Financial Secretary and Secretary of the Women's auxiliary as an adult. Her inspiration comes from her late grandfather, a Baptist preacher, who taught her as a child, "Put your confidence in God, not man." Psalm 118:8.

Beverly Mahone is a journalist with more than 20 years of experience in radio and television. The Canton, Ohio native earned a journalism degree from Ohio University. Her career has taken her to Boston, West Virginia, New Hampshire, Connecticut and Guantanamo Bay Cuba. She continues her television career in Durham, North Carolina while raising her teenage daughter.

Sarah Nkele Matlhare, a native South African is a pharmacy owner in Botswana and the Connectional Chair of Global Housing and Homelessness for the Women's Missionary Society of the African Methodist Episcopal Church. She is the Director of the M. Joan Cousin Empowerment Center, which is located in Lobatse,

Botswana. After coming into contact with HIV patients in her pharmacy on a daily basis, Sarah decided to make a difference in their lives. The center offers seminars, training, counseling, after school tutoring and meals for women and children who were orphaned by the AIDS pandemic.

Patricia Mathis is a native of Cleveland, Ohio and has been a member of DuPage A.M.E. Church since 1979 where she serves as a Trustee, is a member of the Sarah Allen Women's Missionary Society, is a member of the Voices of Praise Choir, and a former member of the Usher Board and takes Isaiah 43:1 as her motto: "Fear not, for I have redeemed you; I have summoned you by name, you are mine."

Michele Matthews is a Contract Administrator in Virginia Beach, Virginia. For the past nine years she has been a member of the Way of Cross, Eternal Life International Ministries in Norfolk where she ministers through the praise dance. She is also the author of *Raymond's Daughters*, which will be published in late 2003. She is mother to two children, Jordan and Kala, and whenever she's stuck in her comfort zone she remembers when Jesus told Peter to "get out of the boat" and she does the same.

Jacquelin S. McCord is the founder and CEO of T. Joy Andrea Publishers. She is a member of the Apostolic Church of God where she is a member of the Sunday School and Women of Faith ministries. She lives in Chicago and is the mother of two daughters and one granddaughter. She is the author and publisher of three books: *When We Get Straight, A Molehill Is A Mountain, Miss America and the Silver Medal* and one for adults: *Fur Coats In My Closet.* All of her books are based on Christian principles and family values.

Thomas L. McDonald, Sr. is a native of Dayton, Tennessee currently living in Chicago. He is a retired chemist, husband and father of two adult children. Rooted and grounded in a Christian tradition, he has imparted wisdom from his mother to his children. She wrote in the family Bible, "God makes a promise, faith believes it, hope anticipates it and patience quietly awaits it."

Trevy A. McDonald, Ph.D., an author, screenwriter, college professor and motivational speaker is a graduate of the University of Wisconsin-Oshkosh and the University of North Carolina at Chapel Hill. She is the author of the novel *Time Will Tell* and co-editor of two scholarly anthologies: *Nature of a Sistuh* and *Building Diverse Communities*. She has also contributed to three devotional Bibles and other anthologies including *Proverbs for the People.* In her work as a motivational speaker she encourages all to cultivate their God given talents and share them with the world. Trevy, a member of Delta Sigma Theta Sorority, Inc., lives in Chicago where she is the President of Reyomi Enterprises, Inc.

Jewel E. Orr-Jones is an Arkansas native currently living in Racine, Wisconsin. Married and the mother of three daughters and grandmother of six, she is a life member of Wayman A.M.E. Church where she holds various offices. Throughout her life she has taught her daughters and grandchildren to put their faith in the Lord.

Norma J. Hearn Phillips, is a teacher in the Detroit Public School System and the widow of Rev. Dr. Robert L. Phillips who served as Presiding Elder of the North District, Michigan Annual Conference. The mother of two daughters and grandmother to four, she is a member of Ebenezer A.M.E. Church and holds life membership in the Women's Missionary Society. Currently the Second Vice President of the Fourth Episcopal District WMS, she has mentored many young women, some who are now in leadership roles.

C.L. Poindexter is a native of Flint, Michigan currently residing in Atlanta. Ms. Poindexter dedicated her life to the Lord at a very early age and was a member of Mt. Olive Missionary Baptist Church in Flint. She is a member of Delta Sigma Theta Sorority, Inc. Ms. Poindexter enjoys a variety of activities, which includes writing. She is currently working on her first novel. Her recipe for living comes from one of the many motivational books her mother has given her over the years: *If I succeed, I will give thanks. If I fail, I will seek his grace.*

Ethel Powell is a native of the Keystone State and a retired school administrator serving as Director of Government Funded Programs. As a missionary for over 30 years, she has been able to reach out to many people—enabling them to help themselves. A life long member of the A.M.E. Church, her favorite scripture is "Commit all you do unto the Lord and your plans will succeed."

B.J. Primus-Cotton, Ed.D. is a native Floridian and retired nurse and educator. She is a wife, the mother of four and grandmother of eight. Her mission work has taken her to Africa where she has evaluated rural health clinics in South Africa. She is the Connectional Chair of the Task Force on HIV/AIDS, Women's Missionary Society, A.M.E. Church.

Mattie Ramsey grew up in Flint, Michigan and was a member of Quinn Chapel A.M.E. Church where she served as a pianist, Sunday School teacher and a steward. She is now a retired Administrative Secretary for the Federal Government. A mother of two sons and one deceased daughter, she has served with her husband in his pastorate for 43 years. She also served in almost every official capacity with the Women's Missionary Society of the A.M.E. church. Her motto has been: "encourage all people to serve the Lord with gladness and He will renew their strength."

Pauline McNeill Rivers, Ph.D. is a native North Carolinian currently residing in Plant City, Florida where she is an organization development consultant with training and experience as a Psychologist.   Raised in the A.M.E. Zion Church and currently a member of Faith Family Outreach Church in Clearwater, Florida, she has been active in various aspects of ministry since her youth, including Sunday School Secretary, Usher, Bible School Instructor, Home Cell Leader, and Nursery Worker. A wife and mother of two sons, her favorite scripture comes from Psalm 5:12, "For surely, O Lord, you bless the righteous; you surround them with your favor as with a shield."

Lorenzo Robertson is a native of Pahokee, FL currently residing in Tampa. He is the author of the best-selling novel, *Detached* and *eclectic essence: poetry for the heart, mind and spirit*. Currently, Robertson is the co-executive director of Operation HOPE, a nonprofit AIDS service organization in St. Petersburg, Florida. He is currently touring with his one man show, *me, myself and i..*

Reverend J. Ricc Rollins, a native of Tampa, FL, is a best selling author, fine art photographer, motivational speaker, award-winning talk show host, pastor and proud father of two. Rollins' first two novels, *Like Breathing* and *Breathe Again*, both received critical acclaim by readers and booksellers alike. He is currently working on the release of his third novel, *Bated Breath* and two collections of sermons and essays entitled, *Private Pain in a Public Place* and *Miracle in your Mess*. Rollins is the pastor of Breath of Life Fellowship Church, an all-affirming ministry serving the Tri-City area.

Nona Skiby is a fifth-generation Canadian who was born in St. Catherine, Ontario, Canada. Her family came to Canada on the Underground Railroad assisted by Harriet Tubman. Throughout her life, Nona chose "non-traditional" careers such as auto repair and printing. She was the first Black Canadian woman letter–carrier in Toronto in the 1980s. Married to a wonderful man of God, who is the light of her life, Nona is the current Canadian Conference Branch Women's Missionary Society President. Her recipe for living is to take her education and God given talents and apply it to the work of the Church.

Dana Burns Smith was born and raised in Houston, Texas in the fear of the Lord. She is a Supervision Officer, mother and has been married for nine years. Her main goals in life are to honor God, her husband and her mother's legacy. Her greatest desire is to be a Godly example for her three daughters as her mother was for her and her two sisters. What she has learned most through life experiences is to be content in whatever state she finds herself.

Joan Stigler is the mother of three and grandmother to six. She has served her local church close to 40 years as a Sunday School teacher, Christian Education Director, Steward and Missionary. As a Missionary, she has served on the local, area and conference branch levels. Her motto to live by is Micah 6:8, "to do justly, love mercy and walk humbly with thy God."

Irma Williams is a native of Arkansas and a retired Accountant/Human Resource professional. She is mother of two sons and one stepdaughter, the grandmother to five and great grandmother to six. Irma has been a member of St. Stephen A.M.E. church for 56 years and president of the Emily E. Vernon, WMS for the past seven years.

Throughout her life she has encouraged her sons, stepdaughter, family, and friends to put their trust in the Lord and let Him guide their path.

Jacqueline Harvey Williams is a retired educator in Chicago, and the mother of two highly successful sons. She sees success in terms of the good a person does in his life time. She is civic-minded, supportive and encouraging to all who know her. Jacqueline is an entrepreneur and life long learner through traveling, reading and engaging in challenging projects.

DeAnne Winey-Ward, is a native of Lake Charles, Louisiana and has made her home New Orleans. She is a Clinical Research Coordinator employed by Louisiana State University Health Sciences Center working for the School of Medicine in the Department of Psychiatry coordinating clinical drug studies. Her present focus since the passing of her daughter is to establish a program for families who have lost a child and cannot afford a traditional burial. DeAnne's recipe for living is: Surrender to the Captain of my ship and allow Him to guide me into a port of miracles and blessings. Surrender thyself wholeheartedly to the Lord and He will lead the way.